WHAT MAKES AN APPLE?

WHAT MAKES AN APPLE?

*Six Conversations about Writing,
Love, Guilt, and Other Pleasures*

AMOS OZ

WITH SHIRA HADAD

Translated by Jessica Cohen

PRINCETON UNIVERSITY PRESS

PRINCETON AND OXFORD

Published by Princeton University Press
41 William Street, Princeton, New Jersey 08540
99 Banbury Road, Oxford OX2 6JX

press.princeton.edu

All Rights Reserved

Library of Congress Cataloging-in-Publication Data
Names: Oz, Amos, 1939–2018, interviewee. | Hadad, Shirah, interviewer. |
Cohen, Jessica (Translator), translator.
Title: What makes an apple? : six conversations about writing, love, guilt, and other pleasures / Amos Oz with Shira Hadad ; translated by Jessica Cohen.
Other titles: Mi-mah ʻasui ha-tapuaḥ. English
Description: Princeton : Princeton University Press, [2022]
Identifiers: LCCN 2021033877 (print) | LCCN 2021033878 (ebook) |
ISBN 9780691219905 (hardback ; acid-free paper) |
ISBN 9780691230276 (paperback ; acid-free paper) |
ISBN 9780691230269 (ebook)
Subjects: LCSH: Oz, Amos, 1939–2018—Interviews. | Authors,
Israeli—20th century—Interviews. | LCGFT: Interviews.
Classification: LCC PJ5054.O9 Z46 2022 (print) | LCC PJ5054.O9 (ebook) |
DDC 892.43/6 [B]—dc23/eng/20211119
LC record available at https://lccn.loc.gov/2021033877
LC ebook record available at https://lccn.loc.gov/2021033878

British Library Cataloging-in-Publication Data is available

Editorial: Anne Savarese and James Collier
Production Editorial: Ellen Foos
Text Design: Carmina Alvarez
Jacket Design: Lauren Michelle Smith
Production: Erin Suydam
Publicity: Jodi Price and Carmen Jimenez
Copyeditor: P. David Hornik

Jacket images: Amoz Oz in Tel Aviv, Israel, March 8, 2013.
ZUMA Press, Inc. / Alamy Stock Photo

This book has been composed in Sabon LT Std

Printed on acid-free paper. ∞

Printed in the United States of America

1 3 5 7 9 10 8 6 4 2

CONTENTS

PREFACE

In the spring of 2014, while I was editing Amos Oz's novel *Judas*, we began to talk. After the book was published that summer, we found that our conversation was not finished. We continued to meet at Amos's home, where we discussed books and writers, inspiration and influence, writing habits and guilt, marriage and parenthood. After a few weeks we moved from the living room to the study, where we placed a tape recorder on the desk between us.

This book results from the dozens of recorded hours we amassed. The conversations are not presented in the order in which they occurred, nor is every chapter a transcription of one single conversation that began and ended on the same day. We often returned to topics that preoccupied us, and we expanded, condensed, and combined separate parts of intersecting conversations. As we worked together, we developed a friendship. The chapters in this book are not journalistic interviews but the product of a continuous dialogue, giving voice to a close friendship formed over an extended period of time.

There were many topics we did not broach at all. Neither of us felt that this book should be "comprehensive." Amos's collection of essays, *Dear Zealots*, was published in the summer of 2017. Its three essays partially overlapped with some of our political conversations, which we decided to omit from this book. Some of the more essayistic portions of our talks will be collected in a separate volume for future publication. This was how *What Makes an Apple?* evolved—as a personal and biographical book, one possible portrait of Amos Oz as he became known to me in recent years.

—*Shira Hadad, May 2018*

A Heart Pierced by an Arrow

What motivates you as a writer?

In the schoolyard at the Gymnasia Rehavia high school, in Jerusalem, there was a eucalyptus tree on which someone had carved a heart pierced by an arrow. On the pierced heart, on either side of the arrow, were the names "Gadi" and "Ruthi." I remember that even back then, when I was roughly thirteen, I thought: It must have been Gadi who did that, not Ruthi. Why did he do it? Didn't he know that he loved Ruthi? Didn't she know he loved her? Even then, I think I said to myself: Perhaps some part of him knew that it would pass, that everything passes, that his love would end. He wanted to leave something behind. He wanted there to be a vestige of that love when it was over. And that is a lot like the urge to tell stories, to write stories: to save something from the claws of time and oblivion. That, as well as the desire to give a second chance to something that will never have a second chance. That, too. My impetus to write also includes the desire for things not to be erased, for it not to be as if they had never existed. Not necessarily things that happened to me personally. I was never, for example, hired to live in the attic of an old house and spend hours talking with an old invalid, the way Shmuel Ash was in *Judas*. That did not happen to me. But there were people in Jerusalem who talked a bit like Gershom Wald did. They existed, and now they are gone.

I wanted that to be remembered. That Jerusalem of the fiery intellectuals, who stood with one foot in [Yosef Haim] Brenner and one in the Bible, and another foot in Ben-Gurion's court and yet another in Nietzsche, and another in Dostoevsky.

Do you feel that your motivations for writing have changed over the years, or have they remained essentially similar?

I don't know, Shira. I think they're the same, but I'm not certain. I hardly ever ask myself about my motivations for writing. When I sit here before five a.m., after walking the empty streets, with my first cup of coffee, I never ask myself what the motivation is. I just write.

But do you ask where the story comes from?

Yes. Yes. Sometimes I do, but I don't always find an answer. I'll tell you something related to what you asked. I once translated a Russian poem by Anna Akhmatova, but I translated it from Stephen Berg's English translation, because I don't know any Russian. And this poem touches exactly on your question. I typed it on a typewriter, before there were computers. Here is how the poem ends:

> And sometimes I sit. Here. Frozen sea winds
> Blow through my open windows. I do not get up, I do not
> Shut. I allow the wind to touch me. Freeze.
> Evening twilight or early dawn, the same shimmering
>   cloud-brights.
> A dove pecks a wheat seed from my palm held out,
> And this space, borderless, the whiteness of paper on my
>   writing page—
> A solitary, vague urge lifts my right hand, leads me,
> Far more aged than me, it comes down,
> Blue as an eyelid, godless, and I begin to write.

That's beautiful.

I'm not a translator, but I wanted to translate that poem from English. Perhaps in Russian it's even more beautiful, I don't know.

Every so often I ask myself where the stories come from, and I don't really have an answer. Look, on the one hand I do know, because I've always lived the life of a spy. It's written in *A Tale of Love and Darkness*. I listen to other people's conversations, I watch strangers, and when I'm in line at the doctor's clinic, or the train station, or the airport—I never read the paper. Instead of reading the paper I hear what people are saying, I steal fragments of conversations and complete them myself. Or else I look at clothes, or shoes— shoes always tell me a lot. I look at people. I listen.

My neighbor on Kibbutz Hulda, Meir Sibahi, used to say: "Every time I walk past the window of the room where Amos writes, I stop for a moment, take my comb out and comb my hair, so that if I end up in one of his stories, I'll be neatly groomed." It makes a lot of sense, but that's not how it works with me. Let's say: an apple. Take an apple. What makes an apple? Water, earth, sun, an apple tree, and a bit of fertilizer. But it doesn't look like any of those things. It's made of them but it is not like them. That's how a story is: it certainly is made up of the sum of encounters and experiences and listening.

My initial urge is to guess what I might feel if I were him, or if I were her: What would I think? What would I want? What would I feel ashamed of? What, for example, would I hope that no one in the world should know about me? What would I wear? What would I eat? This urge has always been with me, even before I started writing stories, since childhood. I was an only child and I did not have any friends. My parents would take me to a café on Ben Yehuda Street, in Jerusalem, and they would promise me an ice cream if I sat quietly while they talked with their friends. And ice cream was a rare commodity in Jerusalem in those days. Not because it cost a lot of money but because all of our mothers, across the board, religious and secular, Sephardic and Ashkenazi, believed beyond a shadow of a doubt that ice cream meant a red throat, and a red throat meant inflammation, and inflammation meant flu, and flu is angina, and angina is bronchitis, and bronchitis is pneumonia, and pneumonia is tuberculosis. In short—it's either the ice cream or the child. But still, they did make an exception and offer me an ice cream if I didn't ever interrupt their conversation. And they would talk with their friends there for at least seventy-seven hours without a break. To avoid going crazy from loneliness, I simply began to spy on the people at the other tables. I would steal bits of conversations, I would look and see who was ordering what. Who was paying. I would guess what the relationships between the people around the table were, and, based on their appearance and their body language, I even tried to guess where they came from, what their homes looked like. That is something I do to this day. But it's not that I take a photograph, go back home, develop the picture and there's my story. There are usually many iterations. In *Black Box*, for example, there's a young man who has a habit of scratching his right ear with his left hand, which he reaches behind his head. And someone once asked me where I got that from. Because she also knew someone who scratched his right ear with his left hand behind his head. I told her: I'm almost positive I saw it once and it made an impression, but where did I see it? I couldn't possibly say. It comes from some forgotten memory, not out of thin air, but I have no idea where exactly.

You know what? I'll put it this way: When I'm writing an essay, I usually write because I'm angry. But when I write a story, one of the things that motivate me is curiosity. Insatiable curiosity. I'm fascinated by the idea of getting under other people's skin. And I think that curiosity is not only an essential condition for any intellectual work, it is also a moral virtue. That is also perhaps the moral dimension of literature.

I have an ongoing argument about this with A. B. Yehoshua, who locates the issue of morality at the forefront of literary creation: crime and punishment. I think there is a moral dimension in a different sense: putting yourself for a few hours under another person's skin, or in another person's shoes. It has indirect moral weight, although it's not very heavy, let's not exaggerate. But I truly believe that a curious person is a slightly better partner than a noncurious person, and also a slightly better parent. Don't laugh, but I think that a curious person is even a slightly better driver than a noncurious person, because he asks himself—what's that guy in the other lane capable of suddenly doing? I think a curious person is also a much better lover than a noncurious person.

You speak, justifiably, of curiosity as a humanistic virtue. But there is also a different kind of curiosity, an almost contradictory kind, the kind that motivates a child to pull apart a bird to find out what it looks like inside. In your view, can literature written out of curiosity, which portrays people at their low points, and sometimes touches on sadism, be great literature?

That's true. We mustn't forget that there is also morbid curiosity. We find it in children, also in adults, also in writers. The curiosity of people who crowd around an injured person to see his suffering and derive pleasure from it. Works in which the writer is fascinated and even enchanted by evil, such as Shakespeare's or Celine's, have a moral dimension too. Because they challenge the reader, or stimulate moral antibodies in the reader.

And with you, in your books, is there sometimes that morbid curiosity? I think there is.

Of course there is. For example, in the detailed descriptions of dying in the story "The Way of the Wind." Or in the descriptions of sadism, torture, and abuse in "Crusade." *

You are a very familiar author now, people recognize you. This business of "contact with reality"—has it become more problematic over time?

No. In the places where I watch people, I am rarely recognized. If I go to a restaurant, there are sometimes people who recognize me. If I'm at the university, they recognize me. At the auto-shop or in line for the doctor, almost no one recognizes me. Once in a while someone says, "Aren't you that guy from TV? Didn't you used to be in the Knesset?" It happens. Taxi drivers sometimes. But usually people don't recognize me. Certainly not when I'm overseas. And in recent years, when I go to a foreign city, I no longer go to museums because my knees hurt. I don't go to see the famous sites, either, because I've seen enough. I sit outside at a café, or if it's cold then in a glass-enclosed café patio. I can sit alone for two or three hours looking at strangers. What could be more interesting than that?

And when you get back from the café or from the doctor's office, to your writing desk, do you have regular rituals to do with writing?

Look, I'm not going to tell you everything for the record. If the tape recorder wasn't here, I might say more. Not everything. My main ritual is to have everything in its place. Always, for

---

* "The Way of the Wind" appeared in Oz's first book, *Where the Jackals Howl and Other Stories*. The book *Ad Mavet* was published in English as *Unto Death*, although the title story was renamed "Crusade" in the English translation.

everything to be in its place. It makes my family miserable. Someone gets themselves a cup of coffee—Nily, my daughters, my son, my grandchildren, even guests—they leave it for a minute to take a phone call, and when they come back their coffee is down the drain and the mug is washed and drying upside down on the rack.

It's hard to live like that in a house where children live, or used to live.

They were always getting angry at me. Everything left out is immediately removed: keys, papers, letters, notes, anything on a surface must quickly go into a drawer. No mercy.

Yes, I see how full your drawers are.

Listen, my father was a librarian, my father-in-law was a librarian, my sister-in-law is a librarian, my wife is an archivist. So how else could I have turned out? Even my cat arranges his food in the dish. And if he doesn't, I do.

I don't think I have writing rituals. Maybe in other people I would consider them rituals. For me they're work habits. My day starts early. It's very rare in my life that anything gets written at night. Even if I can't sleep at night, I don't write. Only in the morning. I used to be completely dependent on cigarettes. I couldn't write a single line without smoking, and it was very hard for me to separate writing from smoking, but we got through it.

Do you write in longhand or on a computer?

I handwrite several drafts. I don't copy from one draft to the next, but I write a passage and put it in the drawer, I write it again and put it in the drawer again, and I write another version of the same scene. When there are four or five, sometimes ten versions, I pull them all out, put them in a long line on the desk, and take something from each, and that might be the revised version, the one I type into this computer my-self with two fingers.

And before you write, you take your morning walk.

Yes. Every day, unless it's pouring, or if it's a dusty day like today, when you can't breathe. It helps put things in perspective—what is important? What is not? What will be forgotten in a few days? And what might not be forgotten? I walk even before drinking coffee. I get up, shower, shave, and go out. By four-fifteen I'm outside, quarter to five I'm back, and just before five, when it's still completely dark out-side, I'm already at this desk with a strong cup of coffee. Those are my hours. That's the entire ritual.

Wisława Szymborska has a poem called "Four in the Morning," where she writes: "No one feels good at four in the morning."[1] She's right. Four in the morning is horrible!

Ms. Szymborska, how unfortunate that you and I never met. I would have asked you to have a coffee, I might have shown you the magic of four in the morning, and the coffee would have been on me. I don't suffer, it's not hard for me at four in the morning. I wake up without an alarm clock. On Satur-days and holidays, too. No one calls me on the phone, Nily is asleep, and if there are other people at home they're also asleep. Those are the hours when no one needs me. In Arad I used to go for a walk in the desert before sunrise, because the desert started five minutes from my house. Here in Tel Aviv, I sometimes walk in the little park, or just on the streets, because I find it interesting. The windows are dark, apart from the ones where people leave a light on in the bathroom. A lot of people leave the bathroom light on at night. Maybe they think it'll scare off the thieves. Maybe they leave it in case their child wakes up at night. Maybe they think death won't come if there's a light on in the bathroom.

Once a woman was standing in a lit window at four-thirty a.m., looking out into the dark. I stood there watching her from the dark and I asked myself: What happens to her in these hours? Then she moved away and turned off the light, or perhaps she kept standing there, looking at the dark, and I kept walking, but I walked away with the first kernel of a story. Which I still haven't written. I may write it one day, or I may not.

Besides, sometimes I get to say good morning to the newspaper delivery guy. Now that we're almost at the Days of Awe, sometimes there will be someone going to synagogue very early in the morning to recite *Selichot*,[†] with his phylacteries and prayer shawl in their case. So then it's "Good morning," or if it's Saturday, "Shabbat Shalom," and that's that. I don't stop to talk to people. Not on those morning walks.

Do you think about what you're writing at the time?

Yes, I think about what's waiting for me at my desk. Because I'm almost always in the middle of something. So I think about where I was yesterday, where I left off, where I want to take it.

What I think isn't always what happens, but I do think, and I also somehow bring the people, I bring the characters. For example, that woman Bracha from the story "Curls,"[‡] or her husband, Moshe. This Moshe, he doesn't say more than five or six words in the whole story, and he comes out of it pretty despicably in general. He's physically repellent, too. But the thing is, I knew a little more about him. I know far more about all my characters than I write. About their

---

[†] Prayers of repentance recited early each morning throughout the month of Elul, leading up to Rosh Hashanah.
[‡] "My Curls Have Flown All the Way to China" (*The New Yorker*, September 14, 2015, trans. Maggie Goldberg Bar-Tura).

childhood, their parents, their erotic fantasies. I just don't use everything I know about them. And while I was writing "Curls," I even knew about the other woman Moshe found himself, in Netanya. It was clear to me from the start that it wouldn't be in the story, but I wanted to know a bit more about what happened there, what sort of person he was and what complaints he had about Bracha, because he did have complaints. So it was necessary for me to know that. Not for the story. Just so that there would be enough cloth to cut the dress out of. Something like that.

You've never written about wars, even though you took part in wars. Or rather, wars are present in your books in various ways, but there are no battle scenes.

That's true. I've never written about wars, about the battle-field. I tried, but I couldn't do it. I fought in two wars, the Six-Day War in the Sinai Desert and the Yom Kippur War on the Golan Heights, and I can't write about it.

Did you try?

Yes. I tried to tell a story about it. Fiction of sorts, or per-haps something like reportage, to describe it, to record it. I was absolutely unable to do it. Not even to myself. One of the reasons is that my sharpest memory from the battlefield is the smells. The smells never get through. Not in literature and not in film. Not even in Tolstoy's *War and Peace*, in his descriptions of the Battle of Borodino, or in Remarque's de-scriptions of World War I. And not in movies, either. The terrible stench doesn't come through. And without the smell it just isn't right.

Nothing in the world smells worse than a battlefield. Burn-ing metal and burning rubber and burning corpses and ex-ploded ammunition and feces and urine and smoke and decay—the most stunning thing is the smell. The stench. Yes, you can stand up on stage and say, "You should know, war is a putrid thing," but it won't do anything. There are not enough words in language for the smell. You recently reread *A Tale of Love and Darkness*. There is nothing in there about battlefields. Nothing. There are a few things about the days I spent as a child in the siege on Jerusalem. Twenty people lived in our basement apartment, because it was a basement and it served as a shelter for the whole building. Even that, that aspect of war, of people—not soldiers but civilians, the elderly, children, everyone unbathed, everyone going to the bathroom, crowded into the apartment. The thing most engraved in my memory is how badly it smelled. So I think that in that book I wrote about the smell.

You did. And you wrote about the stench at home in the days after your mother died, when you and your father were secluded in the apartment.

You cannot convey the stench of the battlefield in words, I gave up. But there are two things I might be able to tell you, from the very first hours of the war. In the Six-Day War, I was in Major-General Israel Tal's division, and I was exactly in the spot where, on June 5, 1967, at eight a.m., or five minutes after eight, the code word "red sheet" came over the radio, which meant we had to turn on all the communication networks, because up to then everything had been silent. Then we heard Talik's voice come through: "Advance, advance. Over." It's mythology by now. There must have been fifty tanks in that small area, and all fifty of them started up at the same moment. The noise was unbelievable. Imagine fifty heavy, noisy engines. And I remember saying to myself: No, no, this isn't the war yet, it's not real, this isn't it. And it took me a long time of recollecting and rummaging, after it was all over, to understand what was missing for it to be real. Do you know what was missing?

The music?

Exactly. Because where in my life had I seen dozens of tanks roaring into battle? In the movies. And in the movies it's always accompanied by very dramatic music. Afterwards, still on the first day of the war, in the early hours, I sat with a few people on the sand dunes and we waited; I don't even remember what we were waiting for. And suddenly shells started exploding right around us. And I look up and I see, on the hilltop, four hundred meters away, or maybe only three hundred, strangers in yellow uniforms aiming a mortar at us and firing. I remember that I didn't get scared, I was simply astonished. I was insulted: What is the matter with those people? Have they lost their minds? Are they crazy? Can't they see there are people here? My first impulse was not to drop to the ground, or to flee, or to return fire. No. My first impulse was to call the police: There are some nutcases here shooting at us with live ammunition! The desire to call the police was the last normal and logical thing that happened to me in the war. Everything that came afterwards was insanity.

There have been cinematic adaptations of your books. It must be strange for you to watch them.

There is a sort of glass wall—it looks familiar but it's not mine. Dan Wolman made a film of *My Michael*. That film has aged well. It was made on a joke of a budget but it still holds up. I remember that after I saw it, I said, it's so beautiful and touching, but so peculiar to me: it's as though I composed a violin piece and someone was playing it for me on the piano.

You've never been involved in writing a screenplay based on your book, have you?

I've often been asked to be involved. Natalie Portman, for example, very much wanted me to collaborate on the screenplay for *A Tale of Love and Darkness*. I refused. To me, writing a screenplay is a different art than mine, but perhaps the distance is not as great as I think. Lots of people these days write novels and stories in the present tense, as if they're writing a screenplay. Perhaps that's a sign that those people actually want to write for film. They don't have the means, they have no money to invest, but in fact their eyes are on film and not literature. Maybe those writers see a lot of movies and only read a little literature. I'm not saying there aren't wonderful works written in present tense, in literature too, but the natural time for literature to occur in is the past. That is why it's called a *story* or *history*. Writers have this sort of congenital defect where they're born with their head and neck facing backwards.

I remember at least one story, "Nomad and Viper," from your first book, *Where the Jackals Howl*, which is written in the present tense.

I'm trying to remember. I hardly ever reread my own books. I think the last page in the story "Digging," in *Scenes from Village Life*, is also written in the present. I'm not dogmatic about the grammatical tense of a story. You can tell a story in the present tense, there are also a few fine stories told in the future tense. In A. B. Yehoshua's early stories, if I'm not mistaken, there is one that is partly written in the future, I think it's in *Facing the Forests*. . . . Here it is: the final sentence in the story "A Long Hot Day," from *Facing the Forests*.[2] The whole story is written in the present, but at the end Buli[§] switches to the future. And in fact I also did that, on the last two pages of *My Michael*. I have no dogmatic position on the matter, but I think that even if the story is written in the future, it still looks to the past. Take science fiction. Let's say, a story that takes place in the year 3000, a

---

[§] The nickname of A. B. Yehoshua.

thousand years from now, it will still say: Captain Nemo woke up in the morning. It won't say: Captain Nemo will wake up in the morning. The grammatical past tense is the water in which the fish named literature lives.

Do you really not read your books after they're published?

To read a page you've written is a bit like hearing your voice on a recording: strange, embarrassing. If I sometimes open up a book I wrote, one of two things happens: either it frustrates me because I see that I could have written it better now, or it frustrates me because I feel that I'll never write that well again. In both cases it frustrates me, so why would I read it? The only exception is *The Same Sea*, which I do go back to, because I find it so hard to believe that I wrote it. In fact I don't even treat it as one of my books. I don't know where it came from. It passed through me and came out the other end.

You taught a university course on The Same Sea. Why that book? For the reason you mentioned?

Because it's the only one of my books that I can go back to, even with some enthusiasm. I read it and I'm impressed. It's an immodest thing to say, but I really am surprised when I read it. I think it's well written, that book. I look at it like a cow who gave birth to a seagull.

You don't reread the books you wrote because it frustrates you. But tell me a little about how your attitude toward your books has evolved over time.

There are books that have gained a little distance from me and there are those that have gained a lot. For example, I still get invited sometimes to give readings from *A Tale of Love and Darkness*, so it hasn't grown very far from me, because I read a chapter, or talk about it. I'm sometimes asked to read from *Between Friends.* But if you were to ask me today about, say, *The Hill of Evil Counsel,* I could hardly remember a thing. I remember that it takes place in Jerusalem, that it's a story about childhood, that it's during the British Mandate. More than that, I can no longer recall. Other people remember far better than I do, and sometimes it's embarrassing, because I get a letter from someone who's doing research, or perhaps writing about my books, and she asks me a question, and I reply: "The answer is in the book." And she gets back to me three weeks later and says, "No, there's no answer in the book, it's not there." Because after all these years I can't remember what was in the drafts I got rid of, and what ended up in the book.

It's far, far more interesting to me to read other people's books, whether they write better than I do or not as well as I do. My standards are very arbitrary, and apparently not very politically correct: if I pick up a novel or a story, read twenty pages, and think, "I could have written that," then I consider it not a good book. Only if I read it and think, "I could never have written that," does it count as a good book for me.

Does that happen to you?

Yes, it happens.

With young writers, too?

Yes. When I say, "I could have written that," I don't mean that I would have used the exact same language. Or written about the exact same world. But rather that I could have carried that weight. Or perhaps I would have carried it in a completely different way. But when I come across a book that isn't in my league, then it isn't in my league. And they do exist. There are many of them. In Hebrew literature and in world literature.

Does writing get easier over the years? I have a feeling that in your case the answer is no.

Why?

I've read your books, and that's my sense.

Your sense is correct. People think that if someone has been writing books for fifty years, like I have, then it gets easier with time. That is probably true about almost every profession. A carpenter, if he's making his thirtieth table, it must be easier than the first one. And a hairdresser, on the twentieth haircut, it's easier than the first. Perhaps in research, too, the accumulated experience helps you find shortcuts, you know where to look. With a novel or a story—no. For two reasons: Firstly, I don't want to write the same book twice. There are writers who do that. Mainly with a book that did well, they write it again and again. I don't think I've written the same book twice. But perhaps that's just what I think. And secondly, writing is like driving with one foot on the gas and one on the brakes the whole time. The foot on the gas is made of innocence, excitement, the glee of writing. The foot on the brakes is made of self-awareness and self-criticism. Over the years, when you become more aware of your writing and of yourself, the foot on the brakes gets heavier and heavier and the foot on the gas gets more and more hesitant, and that's very bad, it's very bad for the driver and for the vehicle. Everything you've already written rises up against you. Even self-confidence is not something you acquire over time. It's a bit like saying to a detainee at a police station: "Anything you say may be used against you."

Also, "You have the right to remain silent."

Yes. And I say to myself: Maybe you've written enough, sit down and read. There are so many beautiful books to read, and I really have written a lot. But my hand is drawn to the pen, and the pen to my hand. *Judas* took five years to write, and it's not a long book. Five years with long breaks.

Is that reflected in the ratio between drafts and the book? Meaning, as time goes by, do more pages get left out?

Yes. I write more drafts and throw them out. In *Judas*, chapter 47 is the only chapter that does not occur in the twentieth century but on the day of the Crucifixion. And not even the entire day. It begins while Jesus is dying, which is in the afternoon, according to the New Testament, and ends when Judas hangs himself on the fig tree before the holiday and the Sabbath begin. Meaning, the duration is four or five hours, something like that. I wrote that chapter many times. I remember writing it and ending up with sixty pages. I said: That won't do, it'll sink the whole ship. This isn't a historical novel. So I sat down and wrote it again and I got to eighty pages. I wrote it over and over again. I didn't copy from one draft to another but wrote one, threw it out, wrote it again, threw it out again. I think that chapter was written something between twelve and fifteen times. It is now ten and a half pages, and I think there is no fat. But it's hard. I think it was Chaim Weizmann[¶] who once wrote to someone in a letter, "Forgive me, my dear, for writing you such a long letter, I just don't have the time to compose a short letter now."

I've heard that story about Churchill and about George Bernard Shaw.

All the witty anecdotes in the world have been attributed at some point to George Bernard Shaw, Oscar Wilde, or Mark Twain. All of them.

[¶] The first president of Israel.

Which reminds me that I have to give you back the newspaper clipping you gave me, the shelved sequel to "Fernheim."

Oh, yes. Isn't it a pity that Agnon's daughter, Emunah Yaron, published that?

Why is it a pity? It's interesting.

Well, it's interesting for scholars, but it does nothing to increase Agnon's acclaim.

To my mind it is to his credit that, after writing it, he chose to shelve the story and not publish it. That's difficult.

But he didn't want it to be published. I almost never leave manuscripts. I just don't leave them. I left a few final drafts of manuscripts in handwriting, so the kids would have an inheritance. But earlier drafts, I throw away. Things I started and didn't like, I throw away. Things like "Fernheim sequels"—I throw those away all the time, I leave no trace, because I don't want someone later thinking it would be interesting for scholars and publishing it.

That really is an interesting question, the status of these works that a writer leaves behind. Because writers who really don't want that to happen probably do what you do. They throw them away. The clearest example is Kafka, of course.

Kafka, exactly. If you want something burned, burn it yourself. That's what Max Brod always said, and he was right. You wanted to burn them—who was stopping you? You had a match, you had a burner. Why would you leave it up to me?

Do you ever regret throwing away manuscript pages?

To take a recent example, from my last novel, *Judas*, in the drafts I had lots of pages about Shmuel's childhood, which I hardly used, there was no need. But there were all sorts of stories in there, about why he doesn't love his parents even though they are very devoted to him. I knew a lot about him, about his parents and his betrayal of them, about his parents' betrayals of each other, and their little betrayals of him in his childhood. I think I told you that to me, that is the core of the story: not Christianity, not the question of statehood versus no statehood, but Shmuel's betrayal of his parents. That, to me, is the engine driving the whole story. For one winter, he adopts himself a different father and mother. He betrays his parents. In the drafts there was much more, and in hindsight, it's possible that I took out too much, that I should have left in a little more about his childhood. His and his sister's. To make "the mother of all betrayals" more prominent in this novel of traitors. That's possible, I'm not sure anymore. I haven't read it for a while. But on the other hand, I wanted there to be no unnecessary fat. I told you that I took two very long breaks from writing that book. Two places when I said: This isn't for me, it's too much. It's beyond my strength. In the end of course I made compromises.

Do you remember what those places were?

I remember, yes. Once I put it aside for a year and a half, almost two. It was where Atalia asks Shmuel out for the first time. I just didn't know what would happen between them. I only knew what could absolutely not happen. Absolutely not. I looked, I asked her, I asked Shmuel. Where would they go? What would he tell her? How would he say it? What would she ask him? Would they touch each other? How? When? What could I do with them? And if nothing happened between them, how would I write it? The hardest thing to write might be a scene between a man who wants and a woman who is wanted, or even a man and woman who want each other, but where nothing happens between them. Nothing. *Nada.* I realized I couldn't write it. I couldn't see them. It was like they were both in the room but they'd turned off the light and that was that, I couldn't see anything.

How many days do you sit with that before deciding: Okay, I'm letting it go.

A lot. A lot. Either I sit for an hour or two, and do nothing. Look out the window. Doodle on paper. Or I sit and write a half-page draft and rip it up, because I know it's not right, it doesn't work. But I write many such drafts before I say: We're done, this isn't for me. I struggle. I don't give up quickly. Meaning, I sometimes give up on a draft, or on an attempt, but I don't give up on the essence—not that quickly. And the second place, I've already told you about.

The Crucifixion chapter. It's hard to write a scene that's had so many adaptations and interpretations in literature, and in fact in every form of art.

When I wrote it, I had this feeling: How can I? Who do I think I am? After all, describing the Crucifixion is like—like a painter who is told: Here, draw a vase with flowers. How can he? All the great masters have already drawn a vase with flowers. Or a sunset. There are endless Crucifixions in art, there are thousands of paintings of the Crucifixion, and there are stories, and there are novels, and there are numerous films, and of course before all that there are the powerful depictions in the New Testament. And there are Bach's Passions. And the sculptures. And there is Bulgakov, and Saramago. You can lose your mind. Only when I finished the book did I go and look at Saramago, in *The Gospel According to Jesus Christ,* where the Crucifixion occurs at the beginning of the book and in one more page right at the end. I checked to see what he'd done there. And I'm not ashamed.

I'm not giving out grades, but I'm not ashamed of the Crucifixion I have in chapter 47.

Then when did you take the long break from writing? After
writing those two long versions of the Crucifixion scene? In between them?

No, it was in between them. I started, and I realized it wasn't
working, so I left it, and then on the second break I wrote
all the stories in *Between Friends*, and I wrote a book of essays with my daughter Fania, Professor Fania Oz-Salzberger,
Jews and Words. It took eighteen months before I went back
to *Judas*.

And when you did, was it easier?

When I did I realized I had to compromise. That it wasn't
going to be the way I wanted it.

As an editor, the question of compromise in writing is very interesting to me. When is the answer that you have to keep working, persisting, because a better solution is hiding somewhere,
and when do you have to let it go, to compromise, to move on?
For the good of the book or even the good of the author.

I'll give you another example of a place where I compromised in *Judas*, a very difficult part, at the end, when Shmuel is planning to go to the library to say goodbye to Wald,
and suddenly Wald comes to him. Shmuel is still in Abrava-
nel's room, he's still limping slightly. And Wald comes to him
on crutches. It's a short scene, less than half a page, and in
the end Wald kisses him on the forehead. There, that's a
compromise. I didn't want them to part that way. I wanted
something more powerful. I tried for a long time, many times.
I wrote it over and over again. Most of the drafts were longer than what's in the book, but not any better. It's something Dostoevsky would have done much better than I did,

that parting scene. Chekhov, too. Far better than I did. For example, I really wanted to also have something slightly comical in that scene. I made a compromise.

I remember something William Faulkner said, about how since none of the books he wrote met his standards, he judged them based on which had caused him the most suffering. Like a mother who loves the son who became a criminal more than the son who became a priest. What you say is fascinating, because I've read your book and that is a beautiful scene, Shmuel's farewell to Wald. But, after all, I have no access to these versions you fantasized about.

You know, Shira, in every book there are at least three books: the one you're reading; the one I wrote, which has to be different from the one you're reading; and then there is a third book: the one I would have written if I'd had the strength. If I'd had the wings. That book, the third one, is the best of the three. But in all the world there is no one other than me who knows that third book, and there is no one other than me who grieves for it. All in all, I think it turned out pretty well, that farewell scene, I'm not ashamed of it, but if there'd been something a tiny bit funny, it would have been even better. I don't know, maybe there are writers in the world, artists, who never compromise. I don't know, for example, whether or not Bach compromised. The music he heard in his mind versus the music he wrote. Have you ever been to Leipzig?

No.

I once gave a reading in Leipzig and the next day I had a flight at nine a.m., maybe to Frankfurt, I can't remember, for the next reading. So I got up very early and I went to St. Thomas Church at six-thirty a.m. Outside, in front of the church, there is a statue of Bach, I think it's bronze, and he's wearing a jacket like they wore in the seventeenth century, and under the jacket he has that kind of waistcoat, with one button undone. And I loved that so much, that the sculptor gave him one unfastened button.

In the middle?

Yes, in the middle. Here. As if it was out of carelessness. And I don't know if that's what it was or not, we'll never know. But I liked it. Then I went into the church, and the organ that Bach composed on is there, and one thing immediately struck me: how cold it was in there. The church was not heated, and in Bach's days it certainly wasn't. And it's an enormous space, like being inside a refrigerator. And the man sat there for hours upon hours writing heavenly music. How? At home he couldn't write. He had twenty children, from two wives. Not all of them survived into adulthood, but there were lots of children at home and most were still little. He went to write music in the church for hours and hours. How?

For someone trying to work, being cold in a church is better than loads of little kids at home. I'm pretty sure of that.

I don't know. He needed an organ, I don't believe he had one at home. I stood there for fifteen minutes and I couldn't feel my toes and hands because it was so cold. True, it's not like that year-round. Perhaps on terribly cold days he stayed in bed and didn't compose. But still, he went there when the congregants were not there. Do you know about *The Little Chronicle of Anna Magdalena*? It's written as a sort of diary told from the perspective of Bach's second wife, Anna Magdalena, about her life with Bach. It's such a touching little book. When you read it, you really love her, and if you weren't a feminist, you will be by the end of the book, it's unavoidable. I must show you the poem Pinchas Sadeh wrote, called

"On the Margins of the Little Chronicle of Anna Magdalena." I'll read it to you, it's short:

> My lady, fifty-seven years of age were you, and a widow
>   receiving aid
> When in your slender, neat handwriting you began to write
> The little chronicle of your late husband
> The cantor of St. Thomas Church
> And when you were told that long forgotten
> Was the name of the deceased and his works would never
>   be remembered
> You told yourself that only God knows
> If that shall come to be, or not
> My eminent lady, a man of distant generations,
> After two hundred years and more, sitting in a room
> At midnight and listening to the chorale *Schmücke dich, o
>   liebe Seele*,
> Wishes to tell you that the name of your late cantor husband
> Is lauded now from the rising of the sun to its setting
> And for having been a good woman to him in his life
> My dear lady I kiss your hand.[3]

It's not exactly feminist.

Not at all. On the contrary. Neither is the chronicle. But both
the chronicle and this poem practically demand that this
reader—namely, that I—be a feminist. Because the poet both-
ers to thank Mrs. Bach solely for the greatness of her husband and for her willingness to serve him. And because the
way Anna Magdalena belittles herself in her chronicle is also
a shocking internalization of an age-old social injustice. How
did we get onto this topic? Oh, we were saying how cold it
was in St. Thomas Church, and we said there might be artists in the world who produce something that is exactly what
they wanted, who don't compromise. I thought about Bach.

Perhaps he didn't compromise. What do I know? But for me, I know that without compromising you cannot finish any work. None at all. And you also know that.

There's no doubt.

But that's how it is in everything. People think compromise is a bad word. Mostly enthusiastic young idealists think compromise is something slightly fraudulent, spineless, dishonest, opportunistic. Not to me. To me the word "compromise" is a synonym for "life." And the opposite of compromise is fanaticism and death.

In literature, too. Not only in politics.

In everything. Everything. Don't misinterpret that: when I say "compromise," I'm not saying turn the other cheek. I'm not saying, abrogate yourself. Abrogate yourself to your partner, or your child, or your parents, or the neighbors. I'm saying: try to explore, maybe there is something, a third of the way, or two-thirds, or halfway. And that's how it is in work, too. Things didn't work out the way you wanted? Try to compromise as high as you can, to negotiate. The way [Prime Minister] Levi Eshkol used to. Do you know what Eshkol once said about compromise? He had a wonderful line. He said something like this: Everyone makes fun of me for being a compromiser, and I really am a compromiser. If I don't get what I want, I compromise. And if it's not enough, I compromise again. And if it's still not enough, I compromise for the third time until I get what I want.

Wonderful. Especially in the context of drafts.

And I understand what he meant. I think I do. When he gets into negotiations he names a far higher price than what he's really hoping to get. And then he compromises and compromises, until he gets roughly what he wanted. I think that's what he meant, but I'm not sure.

Assaf Inbari has an essay I like, called "Be Thankful for That Which is Complete," where he writes that finishing the work and saying goodbye to it are the most important creative decisions — and the hardest. Because of the compromise we spoke of, because of the drive to keep polishing endlessly.[4] When do you know that you've finished writing a book?

When I can no longer look at it. And I hand the manuscript in to the editor. Then I know, of course, that it's not the best thing I've ever written. I keep mourning the third book, the one I wasn't able to write, the unborn child. But I feel in that moment that it was the best thing I was capable of writing. It's a sort of mantra, for me: "This is the best I can do at this moment. I once did better things, and in the future—who knows. But for now it's the best I can do." It's not an alibi, I know, you can't take that to the police, or to the critics, but I find it reassuring. "More than this, I cannot do now."

When I write, somewhere deep inside I know that it didn't come out the way I saw and heard it. I know that, a priori. Perhaps from experience. It can't come out exactly the way we wanted it to. But what does? You go abroad for the first time ever. Such excitement, such turmoil, such tension, you don't sleep all night, what if we don't wake up, what if the alarm doesn't ring, and when you get back you know it was lovely and full of experiences and rich, but it wasn't a revelation.

Mostly because we took ourselves there, too.

Yes. That's a wonderful thing you said. Accurate. Both the fact that we took ourselves, but also the fact that what we had in our mind, as always, was a little more. Because we heard, we read, we dreamed, we hoped, we had a little more in our mind.

To me those two things are connected.

Yes, you're right.

Are there places in your life, or areas of your life, where you don't compromise? Where you don't believe in compromising?

Yes. There are a few, but I'm not sure if I want to put them on record. I can tell you, for example, that I've never in my life taken an advance for a book from any publisher. Not even when we left Kibbutz Hulda without a penny and I was forty-seven years old. We had nothing, and then suddenly Am Oved offered me an advance for the next book, and I turned it down. Because an advance necessarily binds me to a date. That's something I've never compromised on. It really scares me to have a deadline. That paralyzes me. When I was a university student it was terrible, that pressure of what would happen if you didn't finish your paper by tomorrow, by the next day. University papers were the last time I worked with a deadline, which is like a roof that's going to fall on your head and pieces of plaster are already crumbling.

You told me there are books or stories that you start and then leave. Is that because they can't get close to that third book you spoke of? Or do you just not like them? All sorts of reasons?

It's like this, Shira. I've worked hard all these years. I used to work many hours a day, now only three or four hours in the morning, but I work every day. Meaning, I don't write books based on bouts of inspiration, as if the muse suddenly comes to me and I sit down and write a book, but then a few years later the muse disappears and I rush off to see a psychiatrist and tell him I have writer's block and I can't write. I've never had that. Neither a psychiatrist nor writer's block. I'm not familiar with that. I always write. But over the decades that I've been writing, I've had many more abortions and miscarriages than births. When does that happen? When do I get a sign that I have to throw it out? If I'm writing and writing and writing, and lots of pages build up, and the characters keep doing everything I want them to. The baby doesn't start kicking me in the belly from inside. Then I realize he's not alive. If things are going so easily—like modeling clay—get in, go out, sit down, get into bed, have sex, it's a sign that something's wrong. When is it right? When do I know the fetus is alive? When it starts resisting me. When I wrote *My Michael* and Hannah pulled me into a scene that wasn't right for her, I told her: Sorry, I'm not writing that, it's not in your character. Then she tells me, in the middle of writing: You shut up and write. You're not going to tell me what is and isn't in my character. So I say: Excuse me, but you're my protagonist, I'm not yours. You work for me, I don't work for you. And she says: Leave me alone. Let me live and don't get in the way. I decide who I am and what I do and what I don't. And I answer her: I'm very sorry, I won't write that, and if you don't like it—go find another writer. Stop bossing me around. This is my book, not yours. And this Hannah keeps insisting, and so do I, and that's when I know the story is alive. But if I write for a month, two months, once even longer, and the characters are too obedient, I realize the fetus is stillborn. It has to be thrown out. I need a new pregnancy.

Have you ever shelved something you worked on for years?

Yes. Two years.

How frustrating.

I didn't shelve it. I destroyed it. I don't shelve. I rip it up into tiny shreds and flush it down the toilet. Because I can't light a fire at home. And I'm afraid to throw it in the trash—pages might fly away, someone might find them, I don't want that.

When did it happen?

In between the car crash I had in '76 and *A Perfect Peace*, which came out in '82 or '83. In between those two things there was something I worked on for two years and nothing came of it. Instead I wrote a little children's story, *Soumchi*.

But do you think that could happen to you now? That you could work on something for two years and let it go? Or would you recognize it earlier?

I hope I would recognize it earlier. I wouldn't struggle for two years. Today I'm a little more stingy with time. I don't know how much time I have left. No one can know. I don't know if what I'm going to tell you now is true, but this is how it seems to me: you know those cartoons, Mickey Mouse, or Tom and Jerry, where the cat walks and walks and walks, gets to a crater and keeps walking, and only falls after a few seconds, because at first he just doesn't realize he's over a crater? When I started writing I was like that cat, I just didn't know what I was doing, where I was going. Today I have much less courage than I had when I wrote my first stories. Even *My Michael*, I don't know if I would have the courage to write that kind of book today.

What do you have instead of courage?

Patience.

Sometimes

Let's talk about men and women. The world has changed a lot in your lifetime when it comes to relationships, and power relations, between women and men. And in recent years those changes seem to be getting faster and more extreme.

When I was a boy, the women kept quiet when the men spoke. Here and there a woman managed to get a word in. That was all. Women served tea, made sure there were enough cookies on the table, enough fruit on the table. At my Uncle Yosef's home, Aunt Zipporah almost never sat at the table, instead always standing slightly behind his chair, at an angle, wearing a little white apron, and made sure no one was missing anything. If Uncle Yosef asked her, she would go and fetch a book or a paper from his desk in the next room. In our home, my mother did sit down. Sometimes she talked: a little, two or three sentences. Other women did not talk. When a woman did speak, it was a strike against her: Why is she talking so much? Why is she interrupting? Unless they were talking about child-rearing—yes. About illness—yes. Because they knew more about that than the men did. Not only their own illnesses, but the children's. Women did talk about that. And about prices. But if the discussion was about Nietzsche, for example, or about the British Mandate and the White Paper, it was clear that women could express agreement with someone else at the table, usually their spouse, and they could even ask questions sometimes, but no more than that. And it wasn't just in my home. That was how it was everywhere I remember: in Jerusalem, at our acquaintances' homes in Tel Aviv, everywhere.

And when you got to the kibbutz?

On Kibbutz Hulda it was completely different. On Hulda women did speak at meetings, sometimes very assertively.

Did that surprise you, when you moved there as a boy?

At first I found it enchanting. The girls in my class talked, including when we sat around on the lawn, they talked all the time. But afterwards I came to see that it was not right. The whole thing was not right: the notion of gender equality on the kibbutz was completely twisted. In fact, when the kibbutzim went through "women's liberation" eighty years ago, it was as if they said to women: "If you dress like a man and behave like a man and work at men's jobs, then we'll accept you as one of us and you'll have equal rights." But that means: no lipstick, no nylon stockings, no makeup, no sensual signals whatsoever. If you give up everything that in the outside world is considered "feminine" or "sensual," in short—if you become a man, then you'll be welcomed as an equal. Just like a Polish Jew who came to Germany a hundred years ago and was told: Get rid of your accent, dress like we do, behave like a German, look like a German, and then maybe we'll accept you as one of us. On the kibbutz they demanded that women give up all the clichés of femininity. I use the word "clichés" because in my opinion these are not necessarily components of femininity. The things they were asked to give up are not things that I in my inner world regard as feminine. Some are, some aren't. But they were at the time, and to some extent still are, the clichés of femininity: lipstick, nylons, heels, jewelry. But at the same time, the men on the kibbutz never dreamed of giving up a single cliché of masculinity. For example, if someone wanted to grow a moustache, he did, and it wouldn't have occurred to anyone to tell him: "You're not allowed to have a moustache here." I will say to these men's credit that if a woman happened to have a slight moustache, they didn't say a word. So what happened was that the women dressed like men, they wore navy-blue work clothes, wide trousers and Israeli-made button-down shirts, and they walked around in heavy men's boots, and then people accepted them even in the secretariat, at meetings, on committees, everything. But sometimes, among themselves, in conversations among men only, I heard the men grumbling about how their women weren't feminine enough or sensual enough. I never heard a man say that to a woman.

There was one woman on Hulda who was close to me, an older woman, one of the founding members. At the end of her life, when she was very ill, she told me, "If I had to live my life over again, I would give up on the committees and the meetings and the public offices, and I would have a piano at home and I would have guests over, and I would cook and paint and be a hostess." And I said to her, "Why did you think you couldn't have both those things?" She did not answer. Instead, she suddenly burst into tears: it had never occurred to her that it wasn't an either-or proposition. I will never forget the way she sobbed. Never. But that is starting to change in today's world, in some places. It hasn't changed enough, but it's changing.

When I looked at my neighbors in Arad, or when I see my neighbors now in Tel Aviv, couples decades younger than me and Nily, I can see that it's a little different. For example, I see fathers changing their babies' diapers. I was probably the only man on Hulda who regularly changed diapers. And I'm not talking about a million years ago, I'm talking about fifty years ago. The only man on Hulda who was not ashamed to hang laundry. We would take the wet clothes in sacks from the kibbutz laundry and hang them out. Other men did it sometimes, but only if their wives were ill or had gone to a class. Because women were allowed to go to classes. But when the woman was at home? Of course not! Why shouldn't she hang the laundry herself? If a lightbulb needed changing, the men did it. That was actually something I wasn't very good at. It probably hasn't changed in the ultra-Orthodox neighborhoods like Bnei Brak or Meah Shearim. Or maybe it has and I'm not aware. Maybe it's changing there too, under the radar. But it leads to painful things as well. For example, to the release of massive anger at the entire male species. Perhaps it's rage that has built up over generations. Rage and insult. Sometimes the rage and insult are channeled into a missionary ideological impulse, here and there even into a fanatical urge, here and there even into gleeful vengeance. Simone de Beauvoir, among others, men and women, claimed there is no difference at all between the sexes. Or that we should revoke, erase, scrub away any differences. And this is where I stop: I cannot go all the way with that, because in my humble opinion there is a difference.

There are entire schools of thought in feminism that actually do emphasize the difference between men and women, but they see it as a source of power, not inferiority. What do you think the difference is?

Like my grandfather, I don't know, I can't define it. But there is one. I know there is. I know from my life experience. I know it as a spouse, I know it as a father of daughters, I know it as a lover, I know there is a difference. I know, and I wrote about it a little in *A Tale of Love and Darkness*. I know, for instance, that a woman's sexuality—usually, I'm generalizing here, and generalizations are always unjust—is to me inestimably richer and more complex than a man's. The difference between a man's sexuality and a woman's sexuality is roughly like the difference between a drum and a violin. In my very subjective opinion, women's sexuality has an advantage in terms of subtlety and sophistication: It's easier to satisfy a man than to satisfy a woman. That's how it is. How do I know that? After all, I've never been a woman. But I look. And perhaps men and women have slightly different ranges of sensitivity and of vulnerability. But I would never say that women are more vulnerable than men.

That's not true.

No. It simply isn't true. But I think the ranges of vulnerability might vary a little. In what way? I'm not sure. Maybe you know better than I do. But that is one of the differences, for example. Everything I've said up to now should be taken with a grain of salt. Because there are millions of women to whom what I just said does not apply, and there are millions of men to whom it doesn't apply, and there are millions of people in the world who identify as neither male nor female.

I think that when the dust settles from the militancy, from the fury that has accumulated over many generations, from the elation of liberation, perhaps even the slight thirst for revenge, when that dust settles, women and men will be able to see one another more clearly than they do today. I will not live to see it, but I hope my children and my grandchildren will. Not that it won't be complicated, it'll always be complicated, even a thousand years from now. That's how it is. Maybe I'm even slightly happy that it's complicated.

That complication certainly provides you with a living. To a great extent, you write about it, about that complication.

It not only gives me a living, it enriches my life, it has enriched my life. And I hope it will enrich the lives of my grandchildren and great-grandchildren, that their lives will also be full of curiosity in all areas, and curiosity about the whole diversity of human sexuality. Perhaps it's already beginning to be clear that we can end the unfairness and establish erotic justice even without angrily erasing the actual existence of gender differences. Perhaps in a few years there will be a relative calm that will enable us all to accept the idea that there can be inter-gender justice, and gender equality, and mutual respect, even without completely eradicating all differences. And not only accepting that idea, but even rejoicing in it. When Simone de Beauvoir taught us that womanhood is a social construct, a programming, a brainwashing, she was certainly right on the essential level of mistreatment and discrimination and injustice. But she was not right at all on another level. Or so I believe. I believe that femininity is not only a construct and masculinity is not only a construct. Hannah Gonen's father in *My Michael* sometimes speaks as if the very existence of two different sexes is a disaster that we must all try to soften. But to me, masculinity, femininity, and the whole fascinating spectrum are not necessarily a disaster. They can be a gift.

You talked about the clear division of roles between men and women when you were a child. But the model you saw at home was not exactly like that. In *A Tale of Love and Darkness* you write that your mother not only sat with the men, but also, as you describe so beautifully, that while she may not have talked much, a single sentence of hers could completely divert the conversation off course.

That is because she was profound, and she was also a very suggestive person. Men had very strong reactions to almost everything she said. She had that power. It's rare. I've encountered a similar power in three or four people my whole life. No more than that. She had far more to say than most people who were in the room with her, men and women, but she rarely spoke. How much of that stemmed from her not wanting to talk a lot—she only liked to say little, and always concisely—and how much from the fact that those were the rules, that was the world? I don't know. She had the power to make men want with all their might to please her, want for her to be pleased with them. How exactly she did this, I do not know.

You grew up in a narrow and very confined world, erotically speaking.

I grew up in a world without women. The woman who gave birth to me, whom I loved so dearly, who left us when I was twelve-and-a-half, had in fact started growing apart from me long before she killed herself. What she left me regarding women is perhaps a sort of vague and confused sense that a woman is something fragile and vulnerable, something you must touch more carefully than a glass vase, and that a woman is made of dreams, of longings, of sensitivity and pain. That is a very bad legacy. It was as though every woman in the world had an invisible note stuck to her: "Caution: fragile." I had no sisters, I was an only child. My cousins were all boys, and on top of that they sent me to a religious school for boys, called Tahkemuni, which was a little like those Catholic hells described by James Joyce in *A Portrait of the Artist as a Young Man*, or in *Dubliners*. Throughout my childhood I knew far, far less about girls than I knew about American Indians, for example.

That's funny.

It's funny to you. I don't find it funny at all. I read endlessly about Indians and saw loads of movies. There was James Fennimore Cooper, and Mayne Reid, and there were Westerns. So I knew. There was racist nonsense in there, but I had the feeling that I knew about them. About girls—I didn't even know that small amount of warped information. Nothing. There was nothing to read. And what there was, it's probably a good thing I didn't read. When I started at age twelve, more or less, to secretly read the kind of magazines you had to hide under the mattress—I wish I'd never read them. Not only did they not help cure my ignorance, they multiplied the ignorance and the prejudices. What you could learn about girls from those dirty magazines was roughly what you can learn about Jews from Hamas textbooks. Those magazines were written from a mixture of misogyny, contempt, and objectification. And more than that: At school there was an old stone building that had been there since the Turkish rule. The walls were two meters thick. It was effective while Jerusalem was under siege, and when it was being bombed, and it was cool in summer. But inside that heavy building, all two meters of wall, all day, every day, without a break, it was all quaking with hormones. Three or four hundred adolescent boys, twenty teachers, and in the whole building, the whole complex, there was only one woman, a heroine: the school nurse. I wrote about her in *A Tale of Love and Darkness*, and I will not repeat that. At recess we would climb the walls of the girls' school named Lamal, opposite the old Edison Cinema, to see how the extraterrestrials lived. What was in there? And when we found out, we were amazed to see that they also had a water fountain in the yard, just like ours, and that they also played hide-and-seek and tag at recess, just like we did. It was astonishing. Almost inconceivable: There were living creatures on that planet, perhaps even intelligent creatures.

Then came the ballpoint pen. The ballpoint pen, let me tell you, was chapter 1 in my sexual education. The top half of the pen was transparent. I think they were smuggled into Israel by sailors, and they used to sell them for one lira. And there was this boy, I won't say his name because he's still alive, but we had this boy who bought one of those pens and he would rent it out to the other kids for one *mil* per minute. He made his lira back ten times over in a couple of weeks, because we would line up to see that pen. When you held the pen like this, you'd see a pretty blond woman with a large chest, wearing short tennis clothes and holding a tennis racket. But if you turned the pen this way, you'd see the same girl completely naked. Nothing on. We used to line up, and the desperate erection would start long before our turn came to hold that pen for a minute. That was the beginning of my sexual education, that pen.

On top of it all I also had a huge problem with the pen, a mechanical problem, because in the pen you saw large breasts and lovely nipples. I did not yet have that loathsome word, *boobs*, back then. You saw large breasts, lovely nipples, and there was a black triangle but you couldn't see a slit. And I was tormented because I figured, either what the school nurse said in her lecture wasn't true, the whole mechanics she explained was wrong, or else the picture wasn't right. You have no idea how preoccupied this little Archimedes was because he couldn't understand the mechanics of it. Something was completely messed up in the engineering. Something that remained unsolved for me for a long time.

Now I'll tell you something bad. Not only me, but all of us, all the boys at Tahkemuni, we were full of hatred, outrage, and bitterness toward the entire female sex. Why? Because the girls had something, we knew they had something, which we wanted so badly to see and they never showed it to us. What did they care? Why? Those misers, they had no mercy, they were heartless. I was so envious of them: a girl could stand at the mirror and look as long as she wants, she didn't have to pay a *mil* for that ballpoint pen, she can just see all that magic whenever she wants to, for however long she wants to. But she won't share it with us. If they would only open the gates of heaven and let us in, they would make us happy for eternity, that's how it seemed when we went to the Edison Cinema. The movies didn't show how it was done, but at the end of every movie it was insinuated that when they did open the gates of heaven, eternal happiness commenced. Why were they cheaping out? Why were they selfish? We hated them. It might have been a bit like the way beggars hate tycoons, or the way homeless people hate homeowners. I thought to myself: If a girl asked me to write an essay for her, wouldn't I do it? If she asked me to risk my life by climbing a tall tree to get down some article of clothing she dropped from the third-floor balcony, wouldn't I do it? I would risk my life and get it for her. If a girl told me to kill a few mafia heads for her, wouldn't I kill the whole mafia for her? I'd do it without blinking. So why won't they do something for us, even though we're willing to do anything for them? They have all the keys to happiness, and they won't even give us a crumb.

The verb "give" discloses a certain profound and deeply rooted distortion, perhaps one of the world's oldest distortions. I feel bad, but I admit that to this day I'm not completely weaned off that basic infrastructure, whereby the keys to all the delights are held by women. And women alone choose—this is an old-fashioned expression that I really like—whether or not to shower me with their favors.

It is a nice expression, but you could argue that it's actually a euphemism for "putting out."

Absolutely. And that's what we grew up on—whether she "puts out" or "doesn't put out." I've learned a few things over the years. For example, when I was a child I was told that if she doesn't "put out," it just means she's unkind and stingy and selfish and egotistical. But if she does "put out" then she's a slut, she's a whore, she's easy, she's beneath contempt. So what do I actually want out of her? I didn't grasp this back then. It took me years to understand, to try and put myself in her shoes. Not only that, but much as I grew up in confinement, so did girls, and perhaps their confinement was far stricter and more difficult than ours was. They were told: "You have a great treasure. If you squander it, you won't have anything to bring to the bridal bed and no one will want you. You can turn into damaged goods in the blink of an eye. Is that worth it to you? It's not. If you waste your treasure, then the best you'll get is factory seconds—a widower or a divorcé, an old or pathetic man. Is that what you want? Whatever they do, you must not give it to them under any circumstances." They also told girls in those days another thing: "If you go crazy and let them have it, a minute later they'll spit on you. They won't want to see you again, you're only worth something to them as long as you haven't given it to them. That's how it goes."

Unfortunately, I think that's sometimes not completely untrue. Of all the distortions you were taught, I'm not sure that one is completely wrong.

Nothing was completely wrong. It was all constructs—today we have a word for it: it was all constructs. What was done to us, and what was done to girls—all constructs. But it's like two different tribes, where the age-old hostility between them comes from pagan rituals, from idolatry. It's true that biology places a burden on girls which it does not put on boys, and that is the risk of getting pregnant. The caution, the complication, the cost—it's not only society that takes the toll. Biology does too. But the fact that biology contains that injustice—how could I have known? Who ever explained that to me? I was completely illiterate, erotically. I was a Neanderthal when it came to girls. I'm sure that if I'd had a sister, I wouldn't have grown up such a Neanderthal. I'm sure that if they'd sent me to a class where there were girls, I wouldn't have grown up such a Neanderthal. I'm sure that if I'd had the opportunity, even two or three times in my whole childhood, to talk to a girl, not necessarily about sex, not about erotics, not about the mechanics, but just to talk with a girl—

About Indians.

About Indians. You know what? Even to play cops and robbers with the girls. Everything would have been different. I grew up on a desert island in many ways, but that way was the most painful, because on the one hand there was the brutal terror of hungry hormones, and on the other, the only means I had to offload that terror was through hatred, fear, hostility, suspicion, and bitterness. Nothing else. And it was all based on ignorance. I was also extremely jealous of the girls, because I was convinced that nothing in them was on fire. My body had turned into a sadistic enemy that tortured me day and night, so badly that sometimes I just wanted to kill it and be done with it. But girls, what fun for them! Nothing in them was burning, no one tortured them the way my body tortured and humiliated me. I was a little idiot, totally ignorant. I lived in an isolated cell, a dark, stifling cell. True, there were also feelings for girls. Not for a specific girl, but for femininity. Actually it wasn't really a feeling, it was a sort of vague longing to feel. And that longing floated on a pink cloud of tenderness, of awe. But I was absolutely forbidden to connect the longing with the woman in the ballpoint pen. At school there was a little synagogue. Going to the synagogue on Yom Kippur and gobbling down a greasy piece of pork would have been easier and less forbidden than bringing the girl from the ballpoint pen to the pink cloud of delicate longings, to the noble feeling.

Did you talk about all this among yourselves?

Yes, but when we did we said horrible things about girls. Hateful things, mockery, dirty jokes, humiliation, completely twisted information, grotesque caricatures of sexual relations, superstitions, nonsensical beliefs. We never talked about how we were distraught, because we didn't even understand the meaning of the word. We didn't know that we were distraught. We didn't know how bad we felt. We only knew that we were full of anger. We were angry males. We perceived sexuality, more or less, as "Pour out your wrath upon the nations." Not just "fuck them," but "fuck the hell out of them." It didn't occur to us that the fact that girls didn't "put out" was in part because we adolescents were all pretty disgusting. We were an excitable herd of horny creatures, replete with fantasies in which we subjugated the girls, humiliated them, screwed them, nailed them, did them. Our entire dictionary of sex was composed of dozens of violent and hateful verbs. Why should the girls have let us do anything?

In fact what you encountered as a child is closer to pornography than to eroticism. Although the question, of course, is where the border runs.

The border is thinner and more slippery than we presume. I don't think nudity is pornography. But what *is* a problem, in my view? Violence, sadism, humiliation. Even objectification games, if they are consensual, I do not view as wrong. Objectification can be part of sexual play when there is complete consent among the participants. The evil is in coercion or duress. I'll put it differently: what horrifies me is abuse of any kind, including the inclination to mix abuse with sex, even though sometimes it's a fine line. I have no problem with a child seeing animals mating on a computer or televi-

sion screen. I have no problem with that. Generation upon
generation of village children all over the world were used
to seeing animals mate in the farmyard or even in the house,
and not only did it not harm them, but perhaps the opposite. Perhaps it made their adolescent torments a lot easier.

My little Fania, when she was two-and-a-half, maybe
three, asked how children are born, and Nily explained to
her. A few weeks later she came to us and asked how children
are born, so Nily said, "But I already told you," and Fania
said, "I forgot." Apparently it didn't shock her or damage
her tender soul. Otherwise she might not have forgotten and
asked us again. I think it would have hurt her very much to
see Mom hit Dad, or Dad hit Mom. Or if she'd heard Dad
tell Mom, or Mom tell Dad, something that made them cry
from hurt feelings or pain; that could be a wound for life.
I have no problem with a child seeing one sexual organ en-
tering another sexual organ. As long as it has nothing to do
with abuse, coercion, insult, use of force, or pain.

It's hard to demarcate that line. Almost impossible.

True. But we must try. I can't tell you exactly where it runs.
I'm not sure I could draw it—actually, I could, but it would
be slightly arbitrary, like any line in the world. But what else
is new? Every line in the world is arbitrary. When the speed
limit is 90 kilometers per hour, what's going to happen if I
go 91 or 92? Is that more dangerous? If a teacher at the
school where your son will soon go tells him he can have
the top button unfastened on his shirt, but not four buttons—
what difference does it make if it's one button or two? Two
or three? There are no nonarbitrary borders. I think we have
to draw the border somewhere, draw a border between sex
and abuse, sex and humiliation, sex and exploitation, sex
and debasement. And that border runs, more or less, along

the line between consent and coercion. True, that line is not always sharp enough either. But the best I can suggest is that we make an effort to mark that border and define it. Because coercion does not begin and end with physical force. There is a whole arsenal of coercion, there is also blackmail and manipulation and false promises and bribery.

I told you that I grew up in a very puritanical environment and I didn't know what a naked woman looked like until that boy brought the ballpoint pen to school. But no. I was wrong. I did see a naked woman long before the pen. When I was five or six, at the end of World War II, there was a British facility near us where they held Italian prisoners of war. We used to throw things at them, as if they were monkeys in a cage. We threw candy and peanuts and oranges at those Italians behind the barbed-wire fence. And one Italian man showed me a picture of a woman, I'll never forget it, a very fat woman, wearing only socks and garters, nothing else. When I saw that I ran away, and for years and years I did not stop running away from that picture. It's a pity. I shouldn't have run. Why did I? Because I'd already been ruined. I'd been told things I should not have been told. And I hadn't been told things I should have been. As far as I'm concerned, the Ministry of Education can give every kindergartener colored pictures showing a naked man and a naked woman. It won't hurt them. On the contrary. These are things I believe today, especially in the context of militant feminism, which has superseded the puritanism we used to have. Although, in fact, those extremes sometimes join together. Both in the religious traditional puritanism, where everything to do with sexuality is connected to original sin, and in militant feminism, in the most radical manifestation of which there is a willingness to sacrifice all eroticism on the altar of some other ideal—justice, liberty, equality. The radical feminist from Chicago, Andrea . . .

Dworkin.

Yes. Who claims every penetration is rape. I hate her. I really feel hatred when I think about her. Why? What do you want? What did we do to you? She's no better in my view than all the religious fanatics and all the revolutionary fanatics who view any pleasure as punishment. Instead of hating wrongdoing and hating injustice and hating discrimination, they hate sex. Why? What did sex do to you? We were given such a wonderful gift, as wonderful as light, as wonderful as the ocean, as wonderful as food, even more so. What do you want from this gift? Is it that there are people who pollute it? There are people who pollute light, too, there are people who pollute the air, the ocean. But what do you want of the gift? I'm angry, both about what they put in my head when I was a boy, and about what is done today by militant feminists, by militant political correctness enforcers, and I'm angry at anyone who slanders sex when they actually mean something else, or don't mean something else. I'm not only angry on intellectual grounds, I'm angry mostly because they increase suffering in the world. They increase feelings of shame and guilt. They increase hypocrisy and anxiety. They prevent people from finding some comfort in life. Life is full of pain, and it always ends very badly. So why object to having three or four things that make our life feel better? Why steal them? Or deride them? Why?

You spoke about women's anger at men at the beginning of our conversation, and now you're going back to that. But in my opinion you're skipping too quickly from the revolution to the anger and militancy it created, and which created it, without pausing to note that it is a positive revolution, an essential one. And yes, like any revolution, it is not polite and not precise. It's sometimes exaggerated and sometimes violent. The pendulum does not land swiftly and gently in the right place, but swings forcefully between the polarities. Because that's how revolutions work. I also think you're not taking into account that after thousands of years of oppression and violence and extreme inequality, perhaps a few years of anger are called for.

I get the anger, and sometimes I get it straight in my face, and I have a hard time with it. It scares me and insults me, that anger. Because like any anger, it generalizes, it does not distinguish: it's "us" against "you all." That anger, and the political correctness, frequently take on a ridiculous form of new Victorianism: "Cover the table legs with socks, otherwise men will start having dirty thoughts." A while ago there was a story in the paper about a journalist in France who filed a lawsuit against the newspaper she worked for, even though no one had personally harmed her, there was no personal sexual harassment, but the environment had sexually harassed her: men hung pictures in their offices, or in the hallways, of naked girls, or scantily clad girls, I can't remember exactly. And sometimes those men even said rude words. So she sued the paper and she won, and I wasn't sure I was happy about her winning. Because if we take it a step further, how do we handle an environment in which racist jokes are told? Why is that any better, really? What about an environment where militaristic jokes are told? Or where pictures of killing fields are hung? How is that better?

She's not saying it's better. And since when does one injustice cancel out another? By the way, I can't recall seeing many offices with pictures of killing fields on the wall.

You're a hundred percent right that one injustice doesn't cancel out another. But if the courts are consistent, they will have to impose severe censorship on a part of human nature. I'm not sure I would go that far. When I was very young, I'm sure I sometimes said things that today I would be ashamed of. For example, I used to tell dirty jokes to girls because I was taught that it turned them on. And I believed it. It took me too long to understand how I'd been poisoned. But the fact that someone puts up a calendar with half-naked girls in his office, or completely naked girls? I wouldn't build a legal case out of that and I wouldn't call it "an environment of sexual harassment." I think that holds the danger of fanaticism. I have a nose for fanaticism, and wherever I smell it, I get worried. There is fanatic feminism in the world, and it's not much better than other kinds of fanaticism. Some of it is rooted in a dogmatic refusal to acknowledge that there are differences. Dostoevsky's Dmitri Karamazov, in *The Brothers Karamazov*, says: "Man is too broad, too broad, indeed. I'd have him narrower." Well, I would not. Nor would I narrow down the differences between men and women. I would narrow down and even eliminate the injustice that results from those differences.

But Amos, I wouldn't want to work in an office where pictures of naked women hang in the hallways either. Because those pictures, in some way, diminish me and shame me. Let's put it this way: When I go to see my boss, who is likely to be a man, to ask for a promotion or a raise, because statistically my male colleagues make more than I do, those pictures remind me of my place in the world, they remind me that I am worth less. And then instead of asking for the raise or the promotion, I smile shyly and politely leave the room.

But Shira, would someone say anything to a woman if she sat by the TV, even in public, even during her work break, watching men play basketball because it turns her on? Would anyone say, "Stop putting pictures of sweaty men playing basketball on TV"? Or of poets reading poetry? Or of a skilled rider on his horse? Or of an artisan hunched over his carpentry table? I say this with a question mark, not an exclamation mark. I think that if these demands were taken to their logical end, life would be more meager.

It's not the same, because of the historical context. Think about the ballpoint pen from your school. Think not only about the lust, but about all the hatred and ignorance and humiliation flowing in the ink of that pen. Presenting women as sexual objects, as the objects of desire, was for years a way to restrict their scope of action, to narrow their existence in the public sphere. To tell them: you're good for this, not for other things.

Objectification. You're talking about objectification. Advertisers, for example, constantly objectify attractive men to market products to women, but that objectification is not nudity, because that doesn't usually work. Look at TV commercials—isn't that objectification?

It is. But the fact is that throughout human history the objectification of men has not played a key role, or any role, in limiting their place in the world. There is no real historical problem of women staring at images of good-looking or skilled men riding their horses and therefore thinking they are worth less and deserve less. On the contrary.

In fact what you're saying is that, factually, for all of history, men have exploited women much more than women have exploited men, not only sexually. The statistics are unbalanced.

And perhaps as long as pictures of naked women hang in hallways, that will remain the case.

Here you clarify to me something I really didn't think of. And perhaps the most important thing in that example is that one lustful look from the employer might rob the employee of her remaining confidence, whether he gives her a raise or not. But let's take it one step further. If the courts are consistent, they will have to censor not only pictures of female nudity in public places, but also works of art, including master-pieces. Let's say that boss doesn't have a *Playboy* calendar in his office, but a little sculpture, a reproduction of the Venus de Milo, or a Titian, or a Gauguin.

That's an excellent question. And here we revisit a problematic issue you raised: Where is the line? I can tell you for myself, that the Titian—I don't feel that it debases me. But another woman might feel differently.

And if another woman felt differently, should the boss have to take down the picture or be sued?

I refer you back to exactly what you told me: the line is impossible to draw, yet it is essential that it be drawn.

I agree with you that the line must be drawn here, too, but in this case I have no idea how to do it. Maybe you do. And another thing: The fact that if the checkout girl at the supermarket is a pretty and attractive woman, almost no one will dare call her "honey" anymore, makes me very happy. But if a customer at the supermarket, including me, looks at the checkout girl for one second too long while she scans the items and bags them and adds up the charges—I would not convict the entire male species for that, nor would I propose legislation. True, we men, almost all of us, look at her a second too long. I do too. And if that second is criminalized, I think the world will become an even sadder place. And the world is a rather sad place as it is, sad enough even though we are still not forbidden to look at you for one second too long.

Someone, probably a threatened and hurt man, recently attacked the Me Too movement and accused it of Mc-Carthyism. To me, that is not at all the case. Not at all. Mc-Carthyism was an aggressive move by the powerful majority against the weakened minority. Me Too is in danger of exactly the opposite. It is in danger of sliding down the slippery slope from understandable and justifiable revolutionary zeal to Bolshevik cruelty: victims are allowed to exact punishment without trial, simply because "the weak are always right because they are weak, and because they have suffered so much, and because they have suffered a historic injustice for thousands of years." This revolution is a welcome one, but on its fringes, as with all revolutions, there falls a shadow of fanaticism.

Yet still, your grandchildren are growing up in a much better world than the one you grew up in, in the sense that we are speaking of.

The world is larger than just from here to Rabin Square downtown. A hundred and fifty kilometers from here, where ISIS rules, a twelve-year-old girl is being sold for a pack of cigarettes. Today's world is not just Tel Aviv. In Bnei Brak, practically walking distance from here, a girl is being forced to marry a man who disgusts her, physically and emotionally, but she is handed over to him because he is a great Torah scholar. And not only can she not refuse, she isn't even sure she wants to refuse. Part of her probably wants to refuse and part of her doesn't, part of her thinks this is the way things are supposed to be. Part of her says: I really was meant for him. I'm the prize he deserves for being a Torah prodigy. And he will be the jewel in my crown. That's frightening. And that is in today's world. But at the same time, at least in the environment I live in, and certainly in many other places, you do see wonderful things among young couples, things my mother or Aunt Sonia could never have even dreamed of when they were young girls.

Getting back to my grandchildren—yes, I think they find it easier than my children did, and my children find it easier than Nily did, and Nily finds it much easier than I do, to talk about sex. Once we were in a restaurant in Tel Aviv with our grandchildren, Dean and Nadav, who were in their twenties, and they asked me and Nily, flat out, while we were eating our fish, when was the first time we had sex. I almost fell off my chair. If I'd asked my grandmother a question like that, or even my Don Juan of a grandfather, Alexander, I'd have been swiftly slapped on both cheeks.

The first time, or the last time?

No, they asked about the first time. The last time hasn't happened yet. For me it was an embarrassing moment, but Nily quickly answered for both of us. She answered with humor and grace. I couldn't get a word out: I was completely paralyzed for at least fifteen minutes. The fact that they had no problem asking us, that's something new. And it's not a bad thing. Your son will ask you, prepare yourself. When he's out of diapers he'll start asking.

You say there should be an effort to mark the line between sex and abuse or exploitation, and between consent and coercion. Then let's make that effort.

I think the line between insensitive courting and harassment is not exactly clear-cut. I think the line between stirring erotic play and objectification is not exactly clear-cut. I think the line between frivolous thoughts or conduct and insult and humiliation is not exactly clear-cut. I think the line between a casual or playful light touch and the violation of someone else's physical autonomy is not exactly clear-cut. I think that even the line between rash talk and being offensive is not exactly clear-cut.

Moreover, I think that all these lines change somewhat from time to time, which makes the question of borders even more difficult and complex than it already is.

I know for sure, and I've already told you this, that all borders in the world are arbitrary, and even slightly ridiculous. But the lack of borders is dangerous, destructive, even lethal.

Where, then, does this border run? Maybe it runs exactly along the line of mutual consent. And I know that is not a fixed line. The line of consent may also be moved, as long as it is moved with consent.

True, sometimes Party A is wrong for a moment, or Party B misinterprets the messages he or she receives or imagines he or she is receiving. But that mistake cannot go on for even one millimeter beyond the signal of refusal. Party A and Party B are certainly allowed to consent five times and refuse the sixth time, or the opposite—to refuse five times and consent the sixth time. We're all allowed to play at objectification as much as we want, or to play all sorts of games involving reward and punishment, bribery and remuneration, bargaining, control and obedience, give and take, as long as the game is consensual. And the consent, as I said, is always absolutely a onetime thing. The agreement is valid as long as the consent is. Not even a second longer. I'm not the one who made that up, I'm just emphasizing a few things I learned from other people.

How do you propose identifying, defining, lack of consent?

Here I side with those who are strict to the point of extremism, and even fanaticism: consent between an employer and her subordinate employee, or between a teacher and his student, is not consent even if both sides decide to call it that. Moreover, every word, every gesture, every movement, even an expression of refusal or distaste—are to be taken as a door slammed shut, and sometimes they should be taken as a slap on the cheek.

What do you do if doubts arise among Party A or Party B? After all, perhaps the refusal or the distaste are part of a romantic game? Erotic play? Coquettish play? In my fanatic view, even the slightest doubt, even the shadow of a doubt, must be interpreted as a door being shut. Even if yesterday and the day before yesterday, even if in an hour or two, the door was or is opened a crack, the border must be as decisive as a locked door. The minute the door is shut, that door is shut. And that's that.

I return to your own story, to your adolescence. Because you didn't stay in Jerusalem, at the religious school for boys, your whole life. And when it came to your erotic education, the move to the kibbutz was also a turning point.

After the ignorant hormonal hell of Tahkemuni, I woke up one morning on Kibbutz Hulda. Look, moving abruptly from monastic Jerusalem to a sort of oasis of permissiveness was an emotional and sexual shock of a kind I'd never experienced. During my early days on the kibbutz, I thought I was a Muslim suicide, a *shahid*—a martyr—who'd arrived in paradise and there were his seventy-two beauties, as promised. It started with the way the girls on the kibbutz walked around all summer wearing shorts that only just covered their crotches, with those elastic bands. And when I say "covered their crotches"? Sometimes a diligent observer could even catch a little preview of the crotch itself through the shorts' elastic.

And you could talk to the girls. Not that I knew how, but I saw boys who actually talked with girls. I was stunned. I saw boys who touched girls and nothing happened to them. Even more wonderful and amazing: I saw girls touch boys, even affectionately. I didn't dare. I did not touch a girl and none of them touched me. It was probably six months before

I placed a terrified hand on a girl's shoulder, for the first time in my life, and I suddenly realized it was possible. That flames would not leap out and consume me. I was completely stunned. One of my urges was to get a bomb and blow everyone up.

Really?

Yes, out of envy. They were so happy, those kibbutzniks! They were allowed to do anything! Anything goes! Why was I the only unhappy one? They had everything: Why did I have nothing? And this was in a society that considered itself socialist and believed everyone was equal. I was convinced the boys were getting everything they wanted from the girls. "Getting" and "giving"—again that trap. Maybe it's time for a worldwide campaign to destroy such ignorance. By the way, it wasn't exactly the way I thought it was. Yes, everything was more permissive. But from my perspective, like an extraterrestrial who'd landed there, I was sure they were handing everything out fairly, just like they distributed soap and toothpaste, to everyone—except me, because I was an extraterrestrial. I was so jealous that I both admired and envied them, and wanted to blow them up. ISIS. I don't want to discuss those shorts with the elastic bands anymore. As far as I was concerned, it was "For thou shalt see the land afar off, but thou shalt not go thither."

I also understood very quickly that I was on the bottom rung, that I belonged to the lowest percentile of the erotic proletariat. I'd gone out of the frying pan and into the fire: I'd simply rolled from one ignorance, the Jerusalem kind, to another, the Kibbutz Hulda kind. I thought I understood that all the girls were only attracted to big, strong, tanned, muscular boys with hair all over their bodies, boys who played basketball, boys who could score a soccer goal from sixteen meters away with their left foot, boys who could wring the neck of a chick without batting an eyelid. That was all the girls wanted. Boys who could dance, boys who had no trouble touching them. And that was how I realized that, once again, I had no chance, I was done for. I was like a yeshiva student who wakes up in a strip club. The kibbutz, of course, was no strip club. Far from it. Today I know that the erotics there were so naïve. More like a rehearsal for a folk-singing troupe than an orgy. After all, they'd showered together up till age ten or so, the boys and the girls. But to me that eroticism seemed—I'll borrow a phrase from my protagonist, Shmuel Ash, in *Judas*—to me it seemed beyond reach. The most desirable gift in life was meant only for the superior race, not for a weakling like myself. "The fire is meant only for the cedars, not for the hyssop."* This made my ignorance even more profound, because instead of dispelling it, it added on another layer of preconceptions. More anger, more hurt pride, more bitterness. There was a little voice inside me that thought: Kibbutz? Egalitarian society? There should have been some sort of aid committee here, an erotic committee that would make sure to occasionally give out at least some leftovers to the needy. A special booth for those who receive aid and those who are disadvantaged and lacking in means. Where was this socialism? At least something! A crumb!

Now I will tell you what finally ended my ignorance, what saved me from becoming a psychopath or a miserable pervert or a chronic Peeping Tom.

My erotic education began with books. *Madame Bovary*, *Anna Karenina*, Jane Austen, Virginia Woolf, Emily Brontë. After I read many novels about the inner lives of these heroines, with just a few vague and censored allusions to their physical lives, I reached a state—something like this exists

---

* Refers to a prevalent saying originating in the Babylonian Talmud (Moed Katan 25b): "If fire consumes the cedars, what shall avail the hyssop that grows on the rock?"

when you learn how to drive—where I was almost ready to take the written exam. I was still a long way from being ready for the practical exam. But I suddenly understood. I understood—and in this I was helped by the wonderful gift I'd received from my mother: imagination. When I read those books I began to say to myself—because, after all, I could have been Emma Bovary—think about it, put yourself in her shoes, put yourself under Anna Karenina's dress—not under her dress in the way I was longing for, but under her dress in the psychological sense. I learned from those novels things that I hadn't known or imagined about women, and as happens sometimes when you read good literature, it turns out that the Chinese are not that different and not as far from us as we think, and the medieval people are not that far from us, and even women are not as far from me as I'd previously thought. These aliens began to seem a little less alien and less scary and less infuriating, and maybe even very slightly like me. That was very exciting to me. It was cathartic.

The hatred born of jealousy and misery and hopelessness began to evaporate, the anger began to evaporate. Very slowly, from within the thick fog, all sorts of shapes began to come into focus for me. Why didn't they "put out," for example? Now I knew that it wasn't because they were cruel or selfish. What frightened them? What did they loathe? They'd never told me what they loathed or feared, and they'd certainly never told me what they found pleasant, what enchanted them, what attracted them. Since the death of my mother, and in fact long before her death, no woman had ever talked to me. Neither a woman nor a girl. Never. I owe it all to the books I read. And what I learned from the books brought about a reversal in me. I slowly filled with a vague sort of envy, a nebulous envy of female sexuality, because I understood that it was infinitely richer and more complex than my own, even though in fact I have no right to speak on behalf of all men.

I learned that it is apparently more complicated to arouse her than to arouse me, more complicated to satisfy her than to satisfy me. What little I was able to deduce about female sexuality from the novels I read filled me with a mixture of respect and envy, but there was no longer any bitterness, nor hatred or anger. Like an ISIS fighter who suddenly realizes that the civilization he was so intent on blowing up has something to teach him. And even something worth cherishing. He suddenly realizes that in some senses the enemy resembles him, and in some senses the enemy is even more sophisticated than him, and in some senses very worthy of compassion and sympathy and even respect. And then the question was no longer, as it had been throughout my childhood, "Why don't they put out?" The question from now on was how to make women want to share with me that great happiness that was beyond my reach. I desperately wanted to learn. I was fifteen, and I so badly wanted someone to explain it to me, I wanted to know. I wanted to take part, even. Do you understand what I'm saying? I wanted to be let in. Not just into someone's bed. I wanted something more: to be let in on their secrets. I wanted to be in both roles at once: to be myself and her in bed. Or on the pine needles in the woods at night.

It took many more years for me to learn that everything I thought I'd discovered at fifteen about female sexuality—was only a half-truth. That the range of human sexuality can be far more similar to the range of male sexuality than I thought at the time, when I read *Madame Bovary* and *Anna Karenina*. Those books were written by men, men who knew a thing or two, but still, nineteenth-century men who were also trapped in a clichéd perception of the connection between femininity and gentleness or fragility. And the differences I discovered between female and male sexuality are not fixed ones. Sometimes like the difference between a drum and a violin, but sometimes a duet of drums, or a duet of violins. Sometimes this way and sometimes the other. And it's not that one woman is this way and another woman is not. I learned that what I thought I'd discovered at sixteen from the books I read on Kibbutz Hulda was true and important and new, but it wasn't everything. Over the years I learned more things about femininity, which Anna Karenina and Emma Bovary cannot teach you, nor even Jane Austen or Virginia Woolf. But those books were a first layer, without which I would not have attained my first taste of honey, nor would I have advanced over the years to graduate studies. I won't repeat it, it's written in *Panther in the Basement*. But as my Jerusalem friend's older sister said, the one who caught me trying to peep on her when I was twelve: "Amos, when you know how to ask, you don't need to peep." Over the years I learned that this was also only a half-truth. Often true, but not always.

I learned one more thing, and don't fall off your chair, but I learned that size does matter. The size of your erotic imagination. The size of your empathy. That was one of the most wonderful things that happened to me in my life, this discovery that when it comes to size, the size of one's erotic imagination, of one's inventiveness, of one's originality—in all these, mine was much bigger than those goal-scoring boys' was. You have no idea how that clump of clouds that had shadowed me since childhood began to scatter, and finally the sun shone for me: "Mine is bigger."

What an amazing moment.

It wasn't a moment, it was a process. Almost by chance I uncovered this secret, that the safe can sometimes be unlocked simply by putting the right words together. Not only words. Perhaps I should say melody. I realized that the melody that would turn one person on was completely different than the melody that would turn another person on. And that is a half-truth as well, because the melody that aroused her yesterday is not always the melody that will arouse her tonight. That's how it goes. And the melody that startled her yesterday will not always startle her tomorrow. There is a repertoire that often works wonderfully, but there are other repertoires, too. Including sometimes even the disgusting and primitive and macho repertoires I grew up on, which usually turn out to be dishonest and distorted, but sometimes not. Even they are not completely disgusting. And something else: Descartes wrote that the soul does not sit in the body like a captain in his ship, but rather is enmeshed within it. And, after all, almost everything in the erotic world is some sort of joining of mind and body. To my mind—and perhaps I read this somewhere—the soul resides in the body like a spider in its web.

That is such a beautiful image.

The web is actually part of the spider's body, he creates it from within himself. And this is also something that is usually true, but not always. I think the difference between animal sexuality and human sexuality is the story. Animal sexuality, as far as I know, does not come with a story. Human sexuality is related to a story, even if we don't sit down and tell it before we make love. The story goes through our minds. Even before we've touched each other, a certain story has gone through our minds. And so the days of the story are as long as the days of human sexuality. Long before the alphabet was invented, long, long before there were novels and memoirs and poetry and novellas and short stories in the world. At sixteen or seventeen, this discovery that human sexuality is always enveloped in a story gave me enormous joy. Why? Because it turned out that I wasn't as proletarian as I'd thought. Because when it came to stories, well, hold on a minute: I have something to offer. And I learned that for me, at least, the best thing to do was tell a story. Other boys? Go ahead, score a sixteen-meter goal, that works too. And this is also only true sometimes. The most important word in our whole conversation today is "sometimes."

Remember Babel's story, "My First Fee"? What a lovely story! It's a first-person narrative about a street boy who makes up a sophisticated, heartbreaking story and tells it to a prostitute. The story touches her, or arouses her, or both—until she gives him his first writing fee. That is almost, almost, a story about me.

If I were to mark the edges of the arc of male seduction methods, it would stretch more or less from slaying lions for one's beloved, or serenading her as she stands on her balcony, through everything in the middle, all the way to arguing about music or social justice. Whereas the arc of female seduction sprawls all the way from alluring nudity, or half-nudity, which is even more alluring in my view, through a language of seductive hints, which has a rich syntax, partly verbal, partly physical, a slight tremble of the lips, a flutter, a shadow of a smile, a double-entendre promise, all the way to a fervent argument about social justice or music. The whole spectrum is laid out before us in all the colors of the rainbow, both female and male. It depends who is seducing and who is being seduced. And that, too, is only a half-truth, or less, because we are sometimes one and sometimes the other. That is why all my formulations are worth no more than a heap of rubbish. Just like all kinds of love potions and love drugs and aphrodisiacs: sometimes it works, sometimes it doesn't. Sometimes you don't need them at all. Sometimes, as my friend's sister said, someone who knows how to ask doesn't need to climb up a tree to peep.

Look, I'm not going to ask you what is in your spectrum of seduction, but I will ask—what is not in it?

It's like this: I'm not a hunter. And I no longer envy hunters. I used to. I can fulfill, almost by request, a fairly wide variety of erotic roles. Based on inspiration, or based on a wish. But among the erotic roles I have learned to play, there is none for the hunter. Not because it's wrong; on the contrary, it's an age-old role, as old as human sexuality, perhaps even older. Perhaps animals have it. But that role does not speak to me. I don't want to be a hunter.

You don't want to, or you can't, or both?

Both. The fact that I'm not a hunter is sometimes a disadvantage and sometimes an advantage. The truth is that seduction and being seduced have always fascinated me more than the hunt, far more than the final note of seduction and the acquiescence. I've always thought it pathetic to pick up a great detective novel just to find out who the murderer is on the last page. A reader who peeks at the last page to find out who the murderer is, or how the mystery is solved, taking a shortcut, is a very miserable reader, to my mind.

I'll tell you something, but don't feel bad. My grandmother, Mala, used to read detective novels like that. But she didn't do it to take a shortcut. She would read a little from the beginning, to figure out what was going on in the story, and then she'd skip to the last page to find out what happens in the end, and then she'd be calmer, and she could relax and enjoy reading the book.

You know what, I can understand that too. I even understand the emotional and erotic parallels of that. There is something known as "love in reverse." First thing, fifteen minutes after you meet someone, you jump into bed with them, and then you start getting to know them or falling in love. There's a short story called "Love in Reverse" by

Yehuda Amichai. But if someone's diet consists solely of dessert, I don't envy him. And if that's all someone wants, I certainly don't envy him.

Meaning, the last page.

The last page is wonderful, but it's only wonderful when it comes at the end of the book.

And it's not always wonderful.

Not always.

I'm actually talking about literature now, but we could expand it to our topic.

All right, you can talk about whatever you want, I know what you're talking about. You're talking about literature. But if it is wonderful, the last page, and even if it isn't, either way, if it's only the last page, then it's practically worthless. All the things I love in this life, or almost all of them, are slow things. In food, in reading, in traveling to new places. I'm not a snacker. Unless I'm starving, and that has exceptions, too. It's no coincidence that when I was forced to teach a writing workshop at Ben-Gurion University, I insisted that it be called "Slow Reading Workshop." Our time is almost up.

That's a pity.

No, there's something else. I also have an entire anthology about how to refuse and how to take a refusal. You can refuse or take a refusal angrily, ironically, with hurt feelings, stubbornly, by faking indifference. Or you can refuse gently or with a shrug of the shoulders, or with compassion. And you can accept a refusal in all these ways—painfully, nobly, tenderly, even vengefully. Should I tell you something? I don't like refusals, and I don't like having to refuse. But that fascinates me, too. As does the richness of the refusal, of the disagreement—if you know how to look at it. It used to be the quintessential insult to me if a woman signaled or said: "I don't want you." Over time I grew curious: Why doesn't she want me? What exactly is the thing she doesn't want? Does she not want me ever, or does she not want me today? Or does she want me but there are obstacles in the way? When someone refuses me, I don't feel defeated. I'm not talking about sex now, I'm talking about love, but it applies to sex too.

Over the years I also learned about something that is wonderful to do, and which resembles the delight of surprising a child. It is a pleasure to surprise a child. And that is true in love and true in sex. If you manage to do something that is a bit like surprising a child—for me, at least, it makes me ecstatic. And it doesn't matter if I'm giving or receiving the surprise. It's wonderful to be on either end of a surprise.

I told you, I grew up as an erotic illiterate full of prejudices. I was like millions of men out there who love sex but hate women. Millions of them walk around the world, sweaty, panting, their tongues hanging out. I meet them all the time, in the line at the doctor's clinic, or on army reserve duty, where they were all around me. All they could talk about was how great sex is and how awful women are. All their jokes were variations on those two themes. So many jokes and anecdotes and stories and boasting about the bedroom. Over and over again, how to crack the safe and how to get rid of the body as soon as you're done. I don't want to boast now about how I became some master of love, a total ignoramus up to age forty and now look where he is. That's not what my story is about. What is it about? About insatiable curiosity. Curiosity is also an emotional goldmine. And it is a wonderful erotic quality. Curiosity.

What is the most erotic trait, in your opinion, in a man and in a woman?

The loveliest trait, the most attractive to me, in both a man and a woman, is generosity. Never mind how wrong we were about that when we were young. Today I know that there is no partner more attractive than a generous woman, and I think there is also none more attractive than a generous man. I have no better gift to offer a partner than generosity, curiosity, and insatiable erotic imagination. And no better gifts could be given to me than insatiable curiosity, outpouring generosity, and a rich imagination.

I might have already told you this in a different context. To me, in love, in erotics, in sex, it's not the case that the more you invest the more you get. What is it then? Maybe this: giving is receiving. Meaning, what you give before going to bed, in bed or on the rug, or on the kitchen counter, or on a raft in a river, or standing in the dark stairwell—the gifts you give are not an investment that will pay back double-fold, or triple-fold, or with interest and inflation. It's the complete opposite of so many other realms in life. It's contrary to market laws, contrary to bartering, it's even contrary to most arrangements between couples, which are arrangements based on give-and-take, on teamwork, on a division of labor. But, surprisingly, it does make eroticism resemble parenthood. Because that's exactly how it is in parenthood: giving is receiving. To bestow means to be enriched. And I'm trying to say something about the great miracle of revoking the barrier that nature itself has supposedly erected between people. Perhaps the loveliest expression in the world is the biblical term, *to know*. So far removed from a fuck or a one-night stand. And from sleeping beauties and knights on white horses. A man who knows a woman, and a woman who becomes known to a man and knows him, so much so that their shared act is no longer just a combination of two things, it is not even merely the melding of two bodies, but rather it is an act of love. That's it. That's my chorus.

I'm sorry if this sounds banal, but ultimately your version of erotics is very close to love.

It's not banal at all, what you said. Because there can be all sorts of staircases of eroticism in the world, all sorts of alleyways and passages, boulevards and one-way streets, and traps, but the best place in the whole big city of eroticism is love.

Amos, you're a romantic.

That might be so. In the sense that I do believe that a miracle can sometimes occur between two people. I not only believe it—I know it, I've seen it. It happened to me. And if believing that makes me a romantic, then yes, I am. And if not being a romantic means not believing in that and thinking that in fact eroticism is a sort of negotiation—well, often it really is a negotiation, one that might be successful or less so. A wonderful transaction or a reasonable one or a failed one. Even what I see as the most wonderful part of eroticism cannot be attained without erotic negotiation. All right. But the thing is, sometimes it's good to remember that this negotiation is merely the ladder. If that's romantic, then I'm a romantic. Yes. And I think you are, too. I'm pretty sure.

A Room of Your Own

I'd like to ask you about your last name, which you changed from Klausner to Oz when you left your father's home and moved to the kibbutz, at the age of fourteen-and-a-half. You write briefly about it in *A Tale of Love and Darkness*. How did you choose the name Oz?*

I don't exactly remember, but perhaps when I felt that I was going to leave home, to move to the kibbutz, the thing I lacked most was *oz*. It was like jumping off a diving board in the middle of the night, without knowing if there was any water in the pool. There was an element of wishful thinking in that name. Besides—I'm not sure now about what I'm going to tell you, because it has been more than sixty years—but perhaps I also chose it because the two middle letters in the name Klausner† were a little similar to the letters in Oz. Perhaps, but I'm not certain. It's a name that a fourteen-year-old boy chose, like whistling in the dark. Today I would not have chosen such a strident name.

I wonder which name you would choose today.

Something much quieter. Something a little ordinary, even: Oren. Gal. Even.

---

* The Hebrew word *oz* means courage, might, strength.

† In Hebrew the name Klausner is spelled *kof-lamed-vav-zayin-nun-resh*, and the letters *vav-zayin* are also in Oz.

Amos Oren. Amos Gal. Maybe you'd have been a different man and a different writer if that had been your name. Was the actual decision to change your name something you were clear on?

Yes. Absolutely. When I decided I was breaking away and leaving home, and that I didn't want to belong to them—to the acclaimed professor, or to the man who wanted so badly to be a professor. I did not want to be theirs. I was only sad about Grandpa Alexander: I didn't want to hurt him.

In 1970 you wrote: "I abandoned the Klausners' name solely because I thought that a young man beginning to write should walk on his own two feet and not be carried into literature on the shoulders of giants." In other words, you connected the name-change with writing, with the need to carve out your own space as a young writer. Today you give a slightly different explanation, a more profound one perhaps. Do you remember how they reacted? Your father and his uncle?

Yes. For my father it was very difficult. He was extremely distressed. He said to me, Amos Klausner, that's not a name you throw away. You're an only child. At the time, when I did it, I was an only child. My cousin, Daniel, was murdered by the Nazis, and Uncle Yosef had no children, and Uncle Bezalel had already changed his name to Elitzedek, so who was left? It's only you, he told me. It wasn't easy. Not for me, either. It pained me, what he said about there being no one left to carry on the name Klausner. Afterwards my father remarried, and my sister Marganita and my brother David were born, but I'd changed my name by then.

Did you ever regret it?

No. But I think that while I was writing *A Tale of Love and Darkness* I made amends, because anyone who wants to can find out what there was before Oz. Partial amends. But no, I've never regretted it. When I arrived on the kibbutz I told them that was my name, and two days after my sixteenth birthday I went to the Ministry of the Interior in Ramleh to apply for an identity card, and I used my new name on it.

But on the kibbutz they called you that from the beginning.

Yes. I think that on the kibbutz they didn't even know. Apart from the headmaster, Ozer Huldai, who had my papers. I asked him not to tell the kids, and they didn't even know my birth name. They did somehow know, I have no idea how, but they found out that I was from a Revisionist‡ family. They knew that and so there were some who suspected I was a sort of fifth column, that I'd come to spy. That was really unfair, because I was the biggest lefty on the kibbutz. I'll tell you a secret: on Hulda, in the elections, the whole kibbutz always voted Mapai,§ and they were very proud of the fact that Mapai got a hundred percent of the votes. As soon as the votes were counted, in the evening, they would put a notice up on the board: "Once again, Mapai received a hundred percent of our votes." That's how it was up until the 1960 election, when there was a big scandal, because when they counted the votes they found a single vote for Mapam.¶ The whole kibbutz was up in arms trying to find out who the traitor was. And they couldn't. They suspected Alyushka, they suspected Honzo, but it was me. That was the first election I was eligible to vote in and I simply betrayed them and voted for Mapam and didn't tell anyone. I *was* a sort of fifth column. Today they're no longer with us, those old Hulda members. If they'd known it was me they would have killed me. The first time I voted, I voted for Mapam, and

---

‡ Revisionist Zionism espoused the ideology of Ze'ev Jabotinsky and evolved into Israel's various right-wing movements.

§ The acronym of *Mifleget Poalei Eretz Yisrael*—the Workers Party of the Land of Israel, a precursor to the Israeli Labor Party.

¶ The acronym of *Mifleget HaPoalim HaMeuhedet*—The United Workers Party, which had a more leftist platform and eventually merged into present-day Meretz.

after that for the various others. Shimon Peres and I were friends for almost forty years, but I never voted for him or for his party. And he knew that.

When you moved to the kibbutz, as a youth, you also decided to stop writing stories.

I'd started writing when I was a child. Even before I learned how to write, I used to make up stories and tell them, because it was all I had: I wasn't tall, I wasn't athletic, I wasn't good at school, I didn't know how to dance or make people laugh. The only way I had to impress girls was to tell stories. I would make up stories and tell them in parts. The kids—even the girls—would gather around to hear my stories, because I put a lot of suspense in them, with action and violence. And sometimes even a little romance. As a boy in Jerusalem I would stand up in Penina's kindergarten and tell serial thrillers to the other children, boys and girls. Later, at Tahkemuni, a circle of boys would gather around me at recess, including the ones who beat me up before or after the story because—why not? Maybe because I used fancy words, and that got on their nerves.

Then I started to write, in the back room of the cultural building on the kibbutz. It was very distressing, because I'd left my home in Jerusalem to get away from the whole world of books and writing. When I left my father's home I said, That's it, I don't want to write. I don't want to be an author, I want to be a tall, bronzed tractor driver. It was very important for me to be very tanned, and very tall, so that the girls would finally notice me.

And you failed at that. Not at being suntanned or tall, I mean, but at not writing stories.

I did manage to get a little tanned in the end, but I utterly failed at being tall. And writing stories—that urge was stronger than I was. Stronger than the shame. I would go to the back room at night, the reading room in the cultural building, on the edge of the kibbutz. The other boys went to play basketball or hang out with girls. I didn't stand a chance at basketball or girls, so I would sit there alone in that back room and write all sorts of poems. I was fifteen or sixteen and I was so ashamed. Just as I was ashamed of masturbating, I was ashamed of writing. What are you doing? What are you doing? Are you crazy? You just promised yourself you were done, that you'd never do it again, so what's going on? Again? How long will this go on? But I couldn't stop. In fact, there in that back room, I bid farewell to poetry writing and began to try my hand at prose. Sherwood Anderson freed my writing hand, but that's something I wrote about, I think, in *Love and Darkness*.

When I was in the army I started publishing stories in *Keshet*, which was edited by Aharon Amir. I think I sent him one story and he rejected it. Then I sent him another one, and he sent me back a postcard with six words: "Well done, it's gone to print." Because of that postcard, I always call Aharon Amir—I did this when he was alive and I do it now, after his death—I always call him "my founder and first editor" (because in the newspaper *Davar*, up to its very last day of publication, it always said in the masthead: "Founder and first editor, Berl Katznelson"). Aharon Amir is my founder and first editor.

One of my first stories published in *Keshet* was "The Way of the Wind," which is about a paratrooper who fell onto electrical wires. It was loosely based on a disaster that occurred on the fields of Hulda, during an Independence Day paratroopers' demonstration jump. Maybe three or four years after that story was published, the Ministry of Education included it on the matriculation curriculum. I took my matriculation exams while I was doing my military service. If I'd taken my literature exam a few years later, I might have been tested on that story. I would probably have failed.

I wrote a story and then another one and then another. And I received two or three letters that slightly helped me overcome my fear of being worthless. Dahlia Ravikovitch, whom I did not know, wrote me a very Dahlia-ish letter, which was heartwarming, and it began with the words, "They say you are an extraordinarily young person." Because of her poems and because of that letter, I fell in love with her a little, and that was before I even met her. But I remember cutting out a picture of her from the literature section in the newspaper and keeping it in the pages of her book, *The Love of an Orange*. (I secretly always called Dahlia Ravikovitch "golden apple."** Never "orange," under any circumstances, but always "golden apple.") But I never told her that I was slightly in love with her, and I never told her that she was a golden apple.

When my first stories appeared in print, more than fifty years ago, I went to the kibbutz secretariat and I said: I would like to have one day a week off for writing. A big argument broke out. It was not between good people and bad people, or between enlightened people and ignorant people. Those who opposed my request had two reasons: Firstly, anyone could come and claim to be an artist. And then who would milk the cows? One person would want to take photographs, another would want to dance, yet another would want to make sculptures, one would want to make movies—who would milk the cows?

They also said, and rightly so: We have no means of evaluating who really is an artist and who isn't. If we give Amos time to create, we'll have to give it to anyone who asks, because we have no way of ranking. That was a serious consideration, and I had no answer to it. I couldn't pound my chest with my fists like a silverback and say, "No, but I'm

---

** The Hebrew word for "orange," *tapuz*, is in fact an acronym of *tapuach zahav*—"golden apple."

special, I'm not like everyone else." There was also an old man there—when I say old, I mean he was forty or forty-five, because we all called the founders "old," and they even called themselves old. His name was David Ofer. And he said—I'll never forget this—he said: "Young Amos might be the new Tolstoy. But what does he know about life at the age of twenty-two? Nothing, is what he knows. Nothing. Let him work the fields with us for another twenty, twenty-five years, and then—go ahead and let him sit down and write his *War and Peace* for us." That was a weighty argument. To this day I'm not convinced he didn't have a point.

There were debates, there were appeals, in the end it went all the way to the kibbutz assembly, and the assembly approved one day a week for me, on condition that I committed to working twice as hard on the other days. That was how I got one day a week for writing. On the rest of the days I worked in the fields. Later I became a teacher at the high school, which we called "the continuation grades."

I wrote *My Michael* in the bathroom. Because we were living in a one-and-a-half-room apartment with a bathroom as big as an airplane one. And I didn't sleep for half the night. I would write and smoke in the bathroom until midnight, or one o'clock, however late I could stay up. I would sit on the closed toilet seat, with a Van Gogh art book we got as a gift on my lap, a pad of paper on the book, a Globus pen in one hand, a lit cigarette in the other, and that was how *My Michael* was written. Or at least most of it.

Not infrequently, when people tell me they travel somewhere to find inspiration for writing a book, somewhere with mountains or lakes or forests or on the beach, I remember our tiny bathroom in the Hulda housing development. When *My Michael* was published, I plucked up the courage to go to the secretariat again, and I said: I would like another day in the week for writing, so that I can have two. There was a big discussion again, there was an argument, people said, "It sets a dangerous precedent" and "Other people will want the same thing." But since there was already a little income, the secretariat members said, Fine, let's decide we're adding on a new cottage industry, and so be it. So I got another day for writing. Then another book came out, and another, the kibbutz was getting more income, and in the end I got three writing days, but that was the upper limit. I carried out a crawling annexation—not of territory but of time. Three writing days and another three teaching at the high school, with work duties on top of that, recruitments,[††] night guard shifts, and on holidays—either in the crops on a tractor, or in the fruit orchards.

And you still wrote on the toilet?

No. In '75 or thereabouts, when I was thirty-six, the secretariat of Kibbutz Hulda gave me a little study. A few months before that, an elderly kibbutz member named Giza had died. She'd come from Poland, or rather Galicia, and had never married or had children. Giza was a restrained, elegant woman with neatly cropped gray hair and sharp eyes behind square glasses. The housing committee gave me Giza's monastic furniture for my study. Giza was very fond of me. She diligently attended my book club every Wednesday evening. She even once knitted me a sweater, and she gave me an original painting, a dreary watercolor by some Polish Romantic artist. She also told me some of her secrets, on condition that I swore never to tell anyone or write anything about them, and if I did then I had to completely change the names and details so that no one would ever know it was about her. In fact she longed for me to write her story, but in disguise.

[††] Due to the seasonal fluctuations of agricultural work, there were times when kibbutz members were "recruited" for extra shifts in whichever branch required them.

Because, on the one hand, she was very embarrassed to think that anyone might find out she'd had "a thing" with a married man, twice, but on the other hand she was afraid that in a few years there would be no trace of her life left, that no one in the whole world would know that she'd ever lived, and suffered, and loved, and even had dreams. She was a lonely woman, and I was her heir, in fact. Even though the kibbutz forbade inheritances.

I was always liked by lonely old women. I ran a weekly book club on Hulda, where we read, for example, Agnon's *Only Yesterday*. I'd read it with them and explain things, and the elderly people would come, and Giza was the most enthusiastic, because the book is about Galicia and it stirred memories and emotions in her. She once said to me, "I would be willing to be your mother, and I might even be willing to be your girlfriend. I mean that in the nice sense of the word, not the other sense, I'm sure you understand." I did understand, but I didn't entirely believe the last part. When Giza died she did not leave a will, but it was obvious that I could use her furniture. By the way, that furniture moved with me to Arad and was in my study there until we left. Giza's furniture: her couch and two chairs. Furniture dating from the austerity era. From the fifties. Furniture stamped on the bottom: "*Lakol*—Ministry of Rationing and Supply." And that was how I got my own writing room.

Over time, your books began making money for the kibbutz.

The kibbutz coordinator came to see me once. It was Oded Ofer (the son of David Ofer, who'd said that maybe when I was forty I would be the new Tolstoy but I was still too young to be a writer), and he said he'd reviewed the accounts, and the income from my books was pretty good. He asked delicately if they could send me two elderly members who were too old for physical labor—he wasn't quite sure how I did things, but if they came to help, might it perhaps increase my output? Or not? I said, "Look, Oded, I'm still young and healthy, why don't you put three elderly members in this industry and send me out to the crops?"

When we left the kibbutz, they said: Nily and Amos will not get a departure grant, because Amos is taking an entire industry with him. We went into arbitration. The kibbutz secretariat claimed: "We nurtured him, we gave him time to write, we sent him to university, we invested in him, now he up and leaves along with a whole industry. Fine, we have no objection, but they have to give up their departure grant." A departure grant after thirty years of membership on the kibbutz was a significant sum, it was something like a hundred thousand shekels, and we were penniless. We had nothing. And both of us were almost fifty. I said: No. Because it's true that I got a lot from Hulda, including writing time and a study, and I am grateful for that, but I did not get my writing skills from Hulda. Moreover, this industry is unlike any other, because at times of high pressure, other branches would have recruitments, where members volunteered to work overtime in fruit-picking, or cotton-thinning, or cotton-picking. But in my branch there were never any recruitments. When I was sick no one replaced me, when I worked overtime no one kept a record of it. Besides, if writing books is an industry, then fine, I was willing to spend two months training whoever the kibbutz designated to replace me. In the end the arbitrator determined a compromise: Nily would get a grant, because how was she to blame? But I would give up mine. We parted ways with Kibbutz Hulda on good terms. There was no dispute and no courts. We compromised. But on the kibbutz, this whole business of creative people—I know there were similar problems with sculptors and painters who made art on the kibbutz. There was a real problem of intellectual property. I'm not sure if they've solved it to this day. Whom does the intellectual property actually belong to when the artist is a kibbutz member?

The rights to the books you wrote there are still yours, of course.

The rights are mine, yes. Of course I could have offered to donate all the royalties to the kibbutz, but that didn't seem right to me.

Why did you leave?

Because Daniel was suffocating, literally suffocating on the kibbutz. We had to get away because of what the olive trees and the crop spraying were doing to Daniel's asthma. Later, in Arad, Daniel adopted a cat, and when we went to see the allergist and he heard we had a cat at home, who slept in Daniel's bed, he was horrified. That must stop, he told Daniel. Daniel was seven and the doctor thought he couldn't understand English, so he said to us, in English: "You must choose: either the cat or the boy." There was a silence, and finally Daniel said, "Keep the cat, keep the cat."

It must have been scary, to leave with almost nothing.

It was like jumping off a diving board in the dark, without knowing if there was water in the pool.

Interesting, that's exactly the image you used to describe leaving your father's home at fourteen-and-a-half.

Shira, if I had to give this book a subtitle, it would be, "The Story of a Serial Jumper into Empty Pools." We got a mortgage and loans, and we moved into a house in Arad, which was not an expensive city at the time, and for the first few years I worked at four jobs to make enough money. At the age of forty-seven, we embarked on what young people usually start after their army service. We were a bit like a couple of new immigrants from North Korea: at forty-seven, I wrote a check for the first time, and had the first incredible experience of getting real money right out of the wall with a credit card.

What were those four jobs?

It was like this: I taught at the university in Beersheba as an adjunct, and I taught at Sapir College as an adjunct, and I wrote a weekly column or sometimes two for *Davar*, edited by Hannah Zemer, and I also gave lectures three or four evenings a week, all over Israel. And for one month a year I would travel to the U.S. on speaking engagements, and those were paid well. There were a few hard and scary years, we lived almost in poverty. But I was only forty-seven, I had the energy, and we slowly paid off the mortgage for the house in Arad. Then, without me asking, Ben-Gurion University sent me a letter one day saying I was now a faculty professor and not an adjunct.

You say that you left, or rather ran away, because you had to. But still, were you glad to leave?

Nily was gladder, I was less so. Nily and the kids were unhappy on the kibbutz. I was all right, I had a few friends there and I found it interesting. I also believed in the ideas of the kibbutz, and I still believe in a soft version of some of them. But today I know that the children's communal houses were a terrible place. The truth is, I knew it back then, but I repressed it. If I could do it all over again, I would have left the kibbutz much earlier. Long before Daniel's asthma. I would have left because my daughters were unhappy in the children's houses. And Nily was also unhappy on the kibbutz.

Without getting into your children's private lives, can you say more about that?

There is a story in *Between Friends* that tells it better than anything I could tell you. It's called "Little Boy." The communal children's housing was a Darwinist place. The kibbutz founders thought, as did Rousseau, that man is born benevolent and is only ruined by circumstances. They believed, as does the Christian church, that innocent children are little angels who have not tasted sin, and that the kibbutz children's house would be a paradise of affection and friendliness and generosity. What did they know, those kibbutz founders? They'd never seen children in their lives. They were children themselves. What did they know of what happens when you leave children on their own? You have only to stand outside a kindergarten for five minutes to know very clearly that you cannot do that. They developed a whole theory about how if the children only spent time with one another, it would prevent them from mimicking the negative facets of their parents. But at nights, after the adults said good night and left, the children's house would sometimes turn into the island from *Lord of the Flies*. Woe to the weak. Woe to the sensitive. Woe to the eccentrics. It was a cruel place.

I am ashamed of letting my children grow up in the children's houses. Fania and Galia. When Daniel was six we left the kibbutz, and in fact when he was two he moved into the family home, like all the other children on Hulda did. And I am even more remorseful and ashamed that when the girls were teased, I did not have the courage to intervene and go to war in their defense. I thought that was not done on the kibbutz. Besides, I was very unsure of myself, because I was an outsider, I was not from there. They'd taken me from a very dismal place and given me a home when I had none, and so even when I was a father myself, I still felt that I always had to conduct myself better than everyone.

Even then.

Yes. I knew full well what happened in the children's house to kids who were slightly weak, or slightly unusual. I knew from my own experience. I cannot hide behind the excuse of ignorance, because I'd been through it all. Perhaps even more harshly than my daughters had. I was an outside-boy and I was constantly beaten up. They would beat me up for being white when they were suntanned, for not playing basketball, for writing poetry, for speaking proper Hebrew, for not knowing how to dance. I also got what is known in the army as "preemptive strikes" because, one day, I was going to leave the kibbutz. My two roommates, who both left long before I did, used to beat me up every day because it was obvious that I wouldn't stay on the kibbutz.

That's terrible.

I can't even look my daughters in the eye and say, I didn't know how unhappy you were. Because I did know. If I could turn back time, I would have left the kibbutz years earlier. Even though I personally was fascinated by the kibbutz, in terms of ideology and human nature—I've already spoken about that. The kibbutz was a treasure chest for me, because it is quite possibly the best university for studying human nature. But it was selfish of me to stay there. The truth is, I was also very afraid to leave, because we had nothing, not a penny. Not from my parents, not from Nily's parents, and in fact I had no vocation either: I was a high school teacher with no teaching certificate, because I hadn't studied for one. What could I do? Nily could have been a librarian, perhaps, and I could have taught somewhere where they would take me without a certificate. We were afraid. I didn't know at that time that the day would come when I would write books that made money. I didn't know that. I didn't even dream of it. I was afraid I wouldn't be able to support my family. Today I think perhaps I should have been bold enough to leave much sooner.

There is a range of actions between leaving and not intervening.

I did sometimes intervene, but it didn't do much good. And I wasn't brave enough. I was afraid of fights and quarrels with the other parents.

And it wasn't done in that era. Parents did not intervene.

Parents did not intervene. Look, there were some that did. There were tougher parents than Nily and me who did intervene and kicked up a fuss with the caregiver and the education committee. They would demand to know what was happening: Someone did this to my child, someone did that to my child, this is unacceptable. I didn't do that. I should have, but I didn't.

What emerges from our conversation is a pretty dismal picture of the kibbutz ideology, and in particular the way it was implemented.

The Israeli DNA still retains a few genes from the kibbutz, and I regard them as good genes. Remember Stanley Fischer, who was the governor of the Bank of Israel? He once told a story about how he flew to Cyprus for a weekend with his wife Rhoda, for a vacation. It's two-thirty a.m., Stanley and Rhoda Fischer are standing at the luggage carousel in Limassol, exhausted, waiting for their luggage. An Israeli passenger comes up to them and asks politely, "Excuse me, sir, are you the governor of the Bank of Israel?" Fischer says yes. "Where should I change money? At the airport, or tomorrow at the bank?" I love that so much. People ask me what I love about Israel. It's that. He didn't insult Fischer, he wasn't rude, but he knew that Stanley Fischer worked for him. That wouldn't happen to the governor of the Bank of France, or to the president of the Deutsche Bundesbank. That is the gene that the kibbutzim and their youth movements passed on, and perhaps are still passing on, to Israeli society. I love it. The anarchy, the directness, the chutzpah, the argumentativeness, the lack of hierarchy: "No one's going to tell me what to do." That is the gift of the kibbutz, of that era, of the early waves of immigration. I know, of course, that now we're slaughtering sacred cows. When I wrote *Where the*

Jackals Howl, when I came out against Ben-Gurion during the Lavon Affair, I was full of the glee of killing sacred cows: the kibbutz ethos, the myth of the founding fathers, and so forth. But today when I see a whole swarm of slaughterers descending gleefully on one old cow, the kibbutz, I find myself on the cow's side a little. Not because I worship it—I fully remember the way it kicks and its stench. But at least it gave some pretty good milk.

In recent years, a lot of kibbutzim have been collapsing or going through privatization. Do you think the kibbutz will disappear?

No. There are at least a hundred communal kibbutzim today, which have not been privatized or converted into green neighborhoods. Most still have shared ownership of the means of production, and that was always the core of the social-democratic vision. It is possible that the kibbutz will flourish again one day. There won't be folk dancing in the communal dining room, or lovemaking in the granary at night. That is over. But perhaps there will be a mature version of what the first pioneers tried to do in their immature way. It won't necessarily happen in rural areas, and perhaps it won't even happen in Israel. There might be lots of urban communes in the future, which will try to create something like an extended family, providing security in old age, more mutual reliance, more involvement in child-rearing. In fact they already exist: some of my grandchildren are members of fascinating urban communes.

I don't know about you, but what I see from here, and I also saw it in Arad, is a lot of people who work harder than they have the strength for, in order to make more money than they need, to buy things they don't need, to make an impression on people they don't even like. Some people will get sick of it. Most won't, most will remain competitive, that is human nature. But there will be a sector that will search for an alternative. And that sector may extract from the original kibbutz ideas the notion of a sort of extended family, without changing human nature, without total equality, without nosing around in people's private quarters to see who owns a kettle and who doesn't. The society that managed to conquer the peaks of social injustice was precisely the society that then discovered steep cliffs of existential injustice. What do I mean? In a society that revokes the gaps between a rich girl and a poor girl, the difference between an attractive girl and an unattractive girl stands out even more. What can the unattractive girl do? Go to the equality committee and say, "I also deserve some"? I said girl, but I could just as easily have said boy. These are things that cannot be resolved. And I hope that if one day, in another life, this business of the kibbutz returns, it will be run by grown adults and not by adolescents who don't know the first thing about life. People who understand that you must not touch the fundamental components of human nature, because that doesn't end well. The majority will never want it, but perhaps the minority can be offered slightly different game rules.

Other than leaving the kibbutz, what else would you do differently if you could live your life over again?

I might have invested more in political activism. I would not have run for the Knesset, under any circumstances. I might have invested more in political activism in times when I still thought the scales were tipping, if I knew everything I know today. I'm not sure it would have changed anything; probably not. Here and there I said things I wish I had not said in public. Today I would not say them, or I might say them in a completely different way. There are other things that I regret, which I will not tell you about.

Can you talk about the things you said in public?

Yes. I can give you an example. A few times I wrote and said that when it comes to the occupation, to peace and the future of the territories, our right wing thinks from the gut and our left wing thinks from the brain. I regret saying that. It's a simplistic and incorrect thought. Today I think that both the left and the right think from both the brain and the gut, and sometimes they both think about the occupied territories and about peace from both their brain and their gut at once.

We've reached this topic, somehow, from the funny story about your writing room.

Yes. On the day they gave me my own study, with furniture I'd inherited from Giza, for me the world changed. Because up to then, in order to write everything I wrote, I used to hide in all sorts of places. In the reading room in the back of the cultural building, at night when no one was around, or in the bathroom in our tiny apartment. And then suddenly I had a place where I knew I could shut the door and have a few hours to myself. The world changed. Everything was different. I felt as if I'd won a million dollars in the lottery. I had never believed in muses, never believed in inspiration, I didn't believe in that stuff, but the minute I had a desk and a chair and a door I could shut, it was different. The minute I could, for example, take a few hours' break from writing and leave the papers waiting on my desk, without having to fold them up and stuff them into a cardboard file so that no one would peek, my life changed. Completely. Maybe poets can write in coffee shops, maybe they can write poetry in a sort of trance. Then they sit down and revise. But prose? Writing a novel is like building the whole of Paris out of matchsticks and glue. You can't just do it in your free time, or in one continuous trance. And there are many days, even now, when I'm at my desk by five a.m. and I sit here and nothing happens.

Do you feel guilty on those days?

Today I know that it's part of the work, but for many years I did feel guilty. When the kibbutz gave me two days, and later three, to write, I would get up before five, go to my study, sit there until lunchtime, write four or five sentences and erase two of them. There were days when I wrote four sentences and erased six, two from the day before. And then at twelve I would go to the dining room for lunch and I'd be filled with shame, because to my left sat a man in work clothes who'd already plowed five acres that morning, and to my right a man in work clothes who'd already milked thirty cows, and I'd sit there between them and thank God that no one knew I'd spent all morning writing six lines and erasing three of them. What right did I even have to eat lunch there? I felt terribly guilty. But then I slowly developed a sort of mantra. I said to myself, Amos, what you do is actually similar to a grocer's job: You come to work in the morning, you open up the shop, you sit there and wait for customers. If there are customers, it's a good day. If there aren't, you're still doing your job by sitting there waiting. You have no idea how reassured I was by that mantra.

With your permission, I'd like to adopt that.

I don't sit and read the paper all that time, I don't play cards or anything like that. No chats, no tweets, no emails, no porn, I just sit and wait. Sometimes I listen to music. That mantra reassured me. I don't have to tell you that guilt is a Jewish invention. Our forefathers invented it here in this land. Then came the Christians and marketed it with colossal success all around the world. But we own the patent. I, as a Jew, have terrible guilt at belonging to the nation that invented guilt. At the same time, if a whole day goes by without me feeling guilty, by evening time I feel guilty about that. We are different from the Christians, who also feel plenty of guilt, because we Jews must be the world champions at suffering from guilt without first enjoying the pleasures of sin. I know that should have been a Woody Allen line, but it happened to come to my mind. Sometimes guilt can be a strong engine. People who have guilt are people who suffer, but people who don't are monsters.

Maybe the Buddhists managed to get rid of guilt. I don't know. If they did, I envy them terribly, but only for a moment. After a moment I no longer envy them but almost pity them. Guilt is a bit like good seasoning for almost anything: creation, sex, parenthood, human relationships. A little seasoning. But if someone were to give us a whole plateful of seasoning—help!

When Someone Beats Up
Your Child

I'd like to briefly map out a general outline of the critical recep-
tion of your books. In your first decade and a half as a writer,
Israeli literary criticism embraced you wholeheartedly and awarded
you huge esteem. Within a short while you entered the mainstream,
you became the voice of a generation. Almost no superlative I
could use here would suffice. Then came more difficult years,
critically speaking, followed by another reversal toward the end
of the last century—I think *A Tale of Love and Darkness* was
the unequivocal turning point. I want to first ask you a general
question: How do reviews, good or bad, affect you? How do they
influence you?

The truth?

The truth.

Look, good reviews are great, because we all need reinforce-
ment. I don't know if I need it more than other writers, or
less, but I do need validation. It strengthens me. But bad reviews have a greater effect than good ones. Imagine that
your child goes out to play in the yard on his own and you
stand at the window watching him. Along come some thugs
and beat him up, and you can't even open the window and
yell. You have to stand there watching your kid get beaten
up. That's how it is with bad reviews. Anyone who tells you
otherwise is either made of stuff I do not know or under-

stand, or is being untruthful. Agnon liked to say that the crit-ics didn't understand him and weren't important to him. You remember in *Only Yesterday*, when Shimshon Bloykof, the painter, says to Isaac Kumer: "It is true that an artist does not understand a thing about his work . . ."

". . . but he certainly understands more than his critics."[5]

Dov Sadan has a very nice story about Agnon and the fish. Do you know it?

I don't think so.

Sadan went to visit Agnon one day, they sat in his study on the second floor, and he asked Agnon: What do you think about your critics? Agnon replied: My wife and children are away. Sadan asked: What does that have to do with it? Agnon said: There are some carp in the bathtub and my wife asked me to tend to them; come with me. Sadan could not under-stand the connection, but they went downstairs, and indeed two carp were swimming in the bathtub. Agnon took the plug out, all the water drained, and the fish started flapping around. He put the plug back in, filled the tub, turned to Sadan and said: "As these fish behave between water and water, so do my critics between story and story." That was Agnon. It's a nice thing to say. Do I believe him? No, I don't. I don't believe anyone who says such a thing. It has nothing to do with literature and books, it has to do with every human act. When a person furnishes a new house and re-ceives his first guest, what they say matters to him, even if they are complete strangers. Clothes, shoes, anything. Why were there years when the reviews liked what I wrote and years when they rejected what I wrote? The truth is, I don't know the answer. The simplest answer is that perhaps what I wrote between *My Michael* and *The Same Sea* wasn't good. Perhaps they're right.

I don't think those difficult years began with *My Michael*. It might have been in the mid-seventies, with *Touch the Water, Touch the Wind*, or maybe in the early eighties, with *A Perfect Peace*.

I don't know.

What do you think?

I don't think that everything I wrote between, say, *A Perfect Peace* and *The Same Sea* was bad. Maybe tastes changed, maybe people wanted to hear a new voice, and that is what happened in those years, and then people said: That's refreshing. It could also be that what one reviewer praised too enthusiastically and too consistently provoked another reviewer or two to say, Wait a minute, who is the kingmaker here? But I don't know. Everything I've said here is variations on three words: "I don't know." But it's a fact. What you pointed out is a fact, and it's also a fact that it pained me very much at the time. Today everything seems more distant, I haven't read those books for many years, but at the time it hurt me a lot. I used the allegory of your child being "beaten up" because they really did deliver a beating. I've never fully understood it.

Yigal Schwartz wrote an article that attempted to understand the extreme emotional responses you provoke, as a writer and as an intellectual. I quote: "Amos arouses in the Israeli cultural arena such extreme responses that it is hard to decipher their logic or roots. On the one hand there are displays of love and admiration, and on the other hand—hostility, hatred, repugnance."[6] Aviad Raz published an essay entitled, "Why We Love to Hate Amos Oz: Reflections Following the Latest Collective Attack," in which he writes of "the urge to pop the balloon," and also—I have trouble saying these words—"to burn the wizard."[7]

How do you explain or understand these reactions to you and to your writing?

In between *A Perfect Peace* and *The Same Sea* there were fifteen years of almost complete consensus, not only in Israeli book reviews but also in Israeli academia, that my writing should be dismissed. *To Know a Woman*, say, or, *Don't Call It Night*, were almost universally panned. The . . . hatred—yes, that is the right word—you're asking if I can explain it? Perhaps we ought to consider some not-quite-literary factors. First of all: He's not one of us. He's an alien. We don't even see him in these parts. He's either off on his kibbutz or at the end of the world in Arad. Who does he think he is, sitting atop Mount Sinai talking down to us? So that might be part of it. If I'd lived in Tel Aviv and gone out and met people and socialized. . . . Maybe it's also the fact that he looked pretty good in those years. . . .

Excuse me for smiling.

Why? I didn't say anything sexist.

No, but you switched to talking about yourself in the third person.

He was everywhere and nowhere. In politics, too. What is going on here? Even prime ministers ask to meet with him, and he gets quoted on the radio, in the newspapers. There's almost no leftist movement he isn't in some way centrally involved in. He's at all the big protest rallies in Malchei Israel Square. He's everywhere but he's nowhere. Because he doesn't quite fit in. He doesn't fit in with the post-Zionist left that says the whole Zionist project was a mistake or a crime, and he doesn't fit in with the ones who say, "This'll soon be over, the last person can turn out the lights." But also not with the ones who venerate the holy places and wax poetic about how virtuous we are and how Israel is a light unto the nations. But also not with the ones who say the Arabs share none of the blame and we're at fault for everything. And also not with the ones who say the Arabs are to blame for everything. What sort of a slippery creature is he? Perhaps they really thought that, politically, I was simply trying not to offend anyone, to hedge my bets on these stocks as well as the other ones. And that is not courageous. That is a lack of integrity. Maybe if I'd been standing on the sidelines I would also have interpreted things that way. But that was not what motivated me. I was motivated by a complexity whose roots might have been in my Revisionist upbringing. In almost always having had two pairs of eyes. At least.

Perhaps it also has to do with your rhetoric, your eloquence, which annoys people. It's as if you write and speak too nicely.

Yes, that's true. That really did annoy people, and perhaps rightly so. Why is he talking so fancy? Why is he putting on airs? Does he always wear his finest Sabbath outfit?

Can you understand that?

Yes. In my day we grew up believing that a genuine, tormented author, like Brenner, should be practically tongue-tied, a stutterer. If this person speaks so nicely and sounds so polished, it must not be sincere. I also recall that the word "affected" was used against me many times. I didn't understand that, because the way I spoke was not gilded. At least I don't think it was. But I did speak with precision. And somehow that didn't align with some clichéd perception of an intellectual as someone who cries out a shattered, prophetic exclamation. If it's from the depths of his heart, then it can't be so articulate.

When I did come to Tel Aviv, I didn't wear torn jeans and I didn't have long hair: I had none of the symbols of the sixties' generational rebellion. And among the leftist opposition, people who opposed Golda [Meir] and the annexation [of occupied territories], the prevalent rhetoric was the one used by Amos Keinan: prophetic wrath, anger mingled with mockery and loathing, no holds barred, attack them and lay into them. I did write a few fire-and-brimstone editorials, but mostly I elaborated my position, rather than issue denunciations. If I did denounce, it was by means of analysis. More irony and less sarcasm, perhaps. A lot of people did not like that at all. And on top of all that he sounds fancy, he looks good, he's not one of us, he thinks he's above us.

It sounds as if even you find that man irritating.

He really is irritating. I'm trying to view him from the side for a moment. There was that basic thing we spoke of, where people said: Why always him? The Israeli arena is small, hardly touched by a single ray of sun, so why does that ray always shine on him? He should step aside. There are other people here, too. I really understand that. I imagine myself in that arena, but with someone else standing under the single ray of sunlight—I'm not sure if I would attack him, but I'd be bummed. I'd think to myself: "I deserve something too." Look, I can't give you an honest answer as to whether I really wanted that spot for myself or whether I simply found myself standing in it. I don't know. It could be that deep down inside I was not sorry to be standing there. But I can tell you this: I've never in my life had the urge to be number one. Nor was I. Not at school, or in sports, or in the army, or on the kibbutz fields, or at university. I don't have that in me. I don't have sleepless nights when someone else gets a prize I was nominated for, or when someone else—I don't know—sells more copies than I do. Yes, sometimes I'm envious. Very much so. I envy a writer who writes better than I do, but I never envy a writer who is more "successful" than me. I envy someone who does something that approaches perfection, but never someone who receives more praise. Not at all.

I believe you, but I wonder if others will.

No, they won't. But it has to be said. It's the truth. I have never, not in sixty years at least, never once attacked any author for literary reasons. Political reasons, yes. Let's say Moshe Shamir, or Haim Goury, Nathan Zach, and before that Nathan Alterman and Uri Zvi Greenberg. But on issues of literary "status," I said to myself: That's none of my business. I won't take part in this war between alpha males over the prey or the loot. I won't.

But why not, in fact? Why shouldn't a writer say that another writer's work is not good? That it's outrageous?

I understand criticism. I've written some things about other books. But if I don't like a book, nothing could induce me to write about it. What for? Am I supposed to warn the public against shopping in a certain store because its produce isn't fresh? It's just a book. No one has ever become sick from reading a mediocre book or a bad book. And secondly, even if I did go to the trouble of writing about a book I don't like, I would absolutely not do it with my teeth bared. Of all the terrible and monstrous acts people commit every day all over the world—murder, rape, torture, oppression, humiliation, fraud—writing a book is such an innocent thing. Even if we were to assume that someone wrote a book out of lust for glory or for entirely commercial reasons, simply because they want it to sell—even that is such an innocent crime. *Whose ox have I taken?** What crime have you committed? So you wrote a bad book. Fine. Then the critic can say this book is not good, and explain why it isn't good. But this

---

* Quote from 1 Samuel 12:3.

violent, murderous urge to demolish a writer, to piss on the book? I think some critics bring all that from other areas of their lives into their reviews. It's nothing new, these things existed a century ago. Heine was a lethally sarcastic critic, and there were and still are many others. But I've never understood what pleasure it gives the reviewer. Actually, it might be naïve to say I don't understand the pleasure. But it's a pleasure I've never been capable of enjoying myself. I know how to be satirical, to be cruel, to be biting, but I keep that for politics, because there we're talking about power and we're talking about people who sometimes shed blood. But if a person's only crime is to write a bad book—what do you want from him?

I'm debating my response to the image you used, of warning people against a spoiled product in the grocery store. It's true that book reviews are sometimes cruel and very violent, needlessly so. On the other hand, readers read reviews partly with the expectation, which I find justified, that critics direct them toward what they ought to read and what they ought not to. People don't have much time. The question of which book to invest your time and perhaps your money in is important.

If you're a critic people listen to, write about good books. The fact that there are hardly any literary critics left nowadays is a very sad thing. In the papers it's a disappearing breed. No. Stop. I'm wrong here, because there still are a few good critics left. In the books section of *Haaretz*, in the "Culture and Literature" supplement, and in other supplements. I can't tell you, because I don't know, what the situation online is. Perhaps there are very interesting things about literature, but I'm not there. And it usually doesn't reach me.

There are interesting things happening online. There are fascinating blogs, there are readers' communities, some of which are huge, where people regularly share opinions and thoughts and recommendations. These are not the critics you're talking about, but they are people who are engaged in reading and writing about literature, and they are full of passion and love for books.

What you say reinforces in me some quasi-mystical half-optimism half-hope, that in the future there will be what existed throughout the ages, even before there was literary criticism. A person will read a book and tell another person: You should read this. That's what will happen. That's what is happening now. I think that usually when someone goes into a shop and buys a book, it's not because they read a review in the paper, but because someone whose taste they trust told them: You have to read this book. You have to. That's what used to happen and that's what will happen.

That's true. And it's the kind of movement that the new reading media are good for. For example, on the Kindle there's an option to highlight, to mark passages you like. Like underlining the text. And every so often they show you—2,600 people highlighted this passage.

I would like to see that one day, this highlighting, to see which things people underline. In our book *Jews and Words*, Fania says that reading has come full circle over the course of history: from slate to tablet, from parchment to scrolling. What you've told me opens up a field of dialogue between writer and readers. If a writer wants that dialogue, he or she can answer, or ask questions. I know this from the many letters I receive from readers. For example, letters from religious women who write anonymously. After *A Tale of Love and Darkness*, Yigal Schwartz made a whole book out of it, because more than a thousand letters arrived, and most of them, maybe eighty percent, were not really about my book but said something like this: "Okay. I've listened to your story, now you listen to my story, please." And then the readers would start telling me about their lives.

The book really did have that kind of effect on people.

Part of the deluge of letters after *Love and Darkness* was extremely interesting and extremely moving. People revealed personal stories that were far more tragic and more dramatic than mine. I've kept those letters. They're a treasure. I also started receiving letters from the far corners of the world. I can't pretend that isn't heartwarming. Years ago, a young woman from Seoul wrote to me. She was thirty at the time, and she'd read *My Michael* and wanted to tell me that it was a book about her and that she couldn't understand how I knew her. I didn't know her. Nor could she have known the book's heroine, because there was an age difference of about forty years. I'm also not convinced this woman from Seoul knew much about Jerusalem. Yet still she wrote to me: "This book was written about me, precisely."

What a delight, to get a letter like that.

Yes. It's heartrending. It's a prize, a gift.

Do you write back?

I do. I used to write back to everyone, but that's a little hard for me now. I reply to most letters. Sometimes just two or three lines, but I do reply. So they'll know it arrived, so they'll know I received it, so they'll know I listened. Sometimes a little more.

A Tale of Love and Darkness prompted more letters than any other book.

Yes. *Love and Darkness*, followed by *My Michael*. A great many people responded. With *My Michael*, almost all the responses were from women.

What did they write?

About half of them—I didn't run the numbers, but I think about half—said, "How did you know?" "How could you understand such things?" And the other half said, "You don't understand anything." I will never know which of the women were right, because I have no way of knowing. I wrote *My Michael* when I was twenty-four or twenty-five. The entire book is told in the first person from a woman's point of view, because at the time I was convinced I knew everything about women. Today I wouldn't dare.

I'd like to take you back to the topic we started on, reviews, and the image of your child being beaten up by bullies. The thing is that you yourself are less fond, at least in retrospect, of some of those children. You told me about at least two of your books that you do not like now. Did the criticism of *Black Box* . . .

And *Touch the Water, Touch the Wind.* Those are two books I have less regard for.

Yes. But when you published it, I assume you did like it.

Otherwise I wouldn't have published it.

When did you begin to like it less?

Over time. It didn't happen suddenly, at a certain moment. Over time it seemed to me that I wouldn't have made something like *Black Box* now.

I'm asking whether the criticism, things written about the book, played a part in this change of attitude. Did you, in some way, say to yourself: These are not just thugs beating up a child, but rather, say, readers who understand something about the book's flaws? Or was it an internal process unrelated to the reviews?

I'm not sure, Shira, I'm not sure. It could be. I suppose I was especially attentive to the reviews that told me: Calm down a little, lower the volume. That might have affected me. But those were the minority. The majority really were attacks and sarcasm and mockery, and those did not affect me, they just hurt me, they pained me, but they didn't—you can't learn anything from that. There are critics who always say to Hazaz: Why don't you write like Agnon? And they say to Agnon: Why don't you write like Hazaz? That's unhelpful. It's never been helpful. They said to me: Take an example from this writer, take an example from that writer. That never helped me.

But they weren't just attacks. Even critics who were usually very supportive of you had reservations about *Black Box*. They wrote about the stereotypical representation of Mizrahim, and the anxiety expressed in the novel about the political and ethnic reversal of '77, about the changing hierarchies in Israeli society. When those reviews came out, or perhaps after some time, did you find them simply pugnacious or did you sometimes say to yourself: These critics saw something in the novel that I didn't see while I was writing it?

I think there were two stages. At first I was simply offended by the malice and the sarcasm. And so I didn't really listen to whether there were any substantive arguments hiding behind the malice and the sarcasm. Because if someone says, "You're ugly, you're horrible, you're disgusting, you're a racist, you're unbearable, and you also have a stain on your shirt," then I won't immediately look down at my shirt. Perhaps—it's been more than thirty years since *Black Box*—perhaps later, on second thought . . .

I think it's been exactly thirty years. It came out in '87.

It came out in '87, I started writing it in '84, you're right. Yes, perhaps it happened later, partly because Galia, my younger daughter, also weighed in. Galia has always been the sharpest critic in the family. She told me: You tried to get away from the stereotypes, but you couldn't. Over time it became apparent to me that the book is too sociological, in

the negative sense. Meaning, the characters are too represen-
tational. As a reader, I don't like that. Why did it happen?
What can I say in my defense? It's complicated. Perhaps it
really was an emotional response to the political reversal, to
the change of power relations. But after all, I haven't read
that book for many years. I remember that while I was writing, I developed more and more warmth and understanding
and empathy toward Sommo, and more and more aversion
mingled with compassion toward that childish, arrogant,
emotional cripple, Alex. And I remember—I don't think I'm
wrong—that at the end of the book it is in fact Sommo who
is the good guy. He is the character who brings about the
catharsis at the end. Sommo is the one who writes to the man
who has poisoned his life: "I didn't know you were sick,
come home to me and I'll take care of you." I do remember
that. I do remember that as I was writing, my attitude toward
Sommo changed. At first there might have been a slightly
anthropological gaze, not patronizing in a hostile way,
but patronizing in a sort of thoughtful way: "Yes, I actually
do understand you." And over the course of writing, my approach changed into a sort of esteem, a respect. But that
was something they apparently didn't see, the critics. No one
saw it. Perhaps because the first parts of the book made
readers so annoyed—Mizrahi readers, or readers sensitive
to Ashkenazi condescension—that they didn't even get to
the end, or they did but they weren't able to see that the
whole book had flipped.

I think that readers who reached the end mostly saw the
catharsis of that commune with Boaz, with his mother, who
seems to join the herd of his lovers. In other words, the catharsis you speak of is slightly quiet or oblique compared to "the
Ashkenazi catharsis."

If I recall, it's not the way you said, because the book ends
with Sommo's magnanimity after his wife and his little

daughter have been taken from him and he is left alone. Here. I'll look for the chapter. I'll read you the last page of the book:

By the Grace of G-d
Jerusalem
Conclusion of the Holy Sabbath
9th of Elul, 5736 (4.9.76)

Mr. A. Gideon
Gideon House
Zikhron Yaakov

Mr. Gideon,

By the driver you sent, who is kindly waiting here in my home drinking a cup of coffee, I am returning to you a few lines in reply to your letter of this morning. First of all I must ask you to pardon and forgive me the harsh and un-necessary insults I cast at you in my letter of two days ago, not knowing you were unfortunately desperately ill and in fact on your deathbed. It is written in our texts, "A man should not be blamed for words spoken in grief," and when I wrote to you I was in the grip of a very great grief.

And now we are on the threshold of the Days of Awe during which the gates of repentance and compassion are opened wide. Therefore I suggest that Ilana and Yifat should come back home tomorrow morning and you too should come at once and without delay to receive the appropriate treatment at Hadassah Hospital. And I suggest that you stay with us as our guest, Alexander. And that Boaz should come too of course, because his sacred duty now is to stay close to his father and tend to him on his sickbed. By virtue of your remorse and your suffering and your heroism in the sanctification of the Name on our battlefields, and with the help of the divine Mercy, I believe you will be healed. Until then you must stay here with us. Not with Zakheim, not in a hotel, and I don't care a fig what all sorts of people of un-circumcised heart say behind our backs. Tomorrow morning I am going to explain the whole affair to the Rv. Rabbi Bouskila, whose eyes will doubtless see to the heart of the matter. And I shall ask him to receive you for a meeting as soon as possible and he will not withhold his blessing, which has already done many wonders for the seriously ill. Apart from that I've also phoned a cousin of my sister-in-law who works in Hadassah in Oncology and I've fixed it up so you'll get special treatment there and they'll do everything possible for you, over and above.

One other thing, Alexander. As soon as the driver finishes his coffee and goes back to you with this letter, I'm going to the Western Wall to pray for you there and put a note between the stones that you should recover. It's the days of mercy now. Please be kind enough to tell Ilana and also Boaz this very evening that we've forgiven each other and that I forgive Ilana and I'm sure that Heaven will forgive all of us.

With best wishes for the New Year, and for a perfect recovery, and without a thought for any anger there may have been in the past,

Michael (Michel Sommo)[†]

But they won't go back to him.

That is left open.

I think they won't.

I think so too. But that ending could not have been written by someone who believed that the old "salt of the earth"

[†] Amos Oz, *Black Box*, trans. Nicholas de Lange (Chatto & Windus, 1988), 241–43.

Israelis were good, and the new ones who came to replace them were bad. But not the opposite, either. Sommo is no saint, and there is always something slightly comical about him. Even when he performs an act of kindness, even when he forgives, even when he is willing to absolve everything, there remains a comical element. But everyone in this book has a little of that. Perhaps in all my books. Even in *Judas*, Shmuel Ash is slightly touching and slightly ridiculous, and so is Gershom Wald and even Atalia.

Do you mean that you see a comical side in the other *Black Box* protagonists as well?

Everyone is slightly ridiculous, everyone is slightly childish. Everyone in this book is a little spoiled, each in his or her own way.

So the critics saw the way you ridiculed Sommo, but not Alex or Ilana or Boaz?

That is what they saw, and perhaps I didn't do good work. The strokes might be too broad. When I was writing that book, my point of departure was that they were all fanatical, without exception. All of them. Sommo is fanatical about "Greater Israel" and about doing mitzvahs and his religiosity and the territories; Alex is fanatical about being a control freak on a massive ego trip; and Ilana is fanatical about her right to be happy. The world can fall apart—but she will be happy. She doesn't care whom she has to trample over to get it. Even Boaz is fanatical, with his hippie commune and his insistence that everyone has to love everyone. A fanatic of sixties slogans. I didn't think a single character wasn't a fanatic. Maybe Ilana's sister, the one who writes her weekly letters. Even the lawyer, who is the most comical of all, is a sort of fanatic about property. He doesn't really care who the property belongs to, as long as it is kept intact. But if not a single reader in Israel saw what I see in that book, then I suppose the book is a little defective. Either that, or my reading of it is a little defective.

It's one of your most successful books.

Around a hundred thousand people in Israel read it. But they might have read it for the wrong reasons.

I think people liked the book a lot. Readers enjoyed it a lot.

Yes, the question is what they enjoyed. They might have enjoyed what they saw as the book making fun of this religious Mizrahi who goes around quoting the Bible. Some readers might have thought it was a bit like Ha'Gashash Ha'Hiver.[‡] I'm not certain that the people who bought the book and enjoyed it and spoke highly of it did so for the right reasons. I'm certain that the people who attacked *Black Box* were seeing red. What did they get right? They were correct in saying that a novel should not be too sociological. If some of the readers laughed and enjoyed it for the wrong reasons, and some saw red for the wrong reasons, then I suppose the book got what it deserved, even though it got it for the wrong reasons.

There are books that I would never be able or willing to write again the way I did. But *Black Box*—I think today I could make it into something a little better. Were my eyes opened by the dreadful reviews? By the few compliments, which were accompanied by completely erroneous arguments, in my view? After I was done being insulted by the reviews, and done being hurt, and done being bitter and feeling bad, perhaps I did learn something.

By the way, Shira, if you have a better explanation for why those years, not only around *Black Box*, but why that whole

---

[‡] A famous and beloved Israeli comedy trio, known for their satirical portrayals of ubiquitous Israeli characters.

period was one of wall-to-wall hostility, I would like to hear it, because I am not the best person to explain these things. When someone hits you, it's no good to ask you why you got hit. You have to ask the hitters. Look, I'm not a victim, not at all. But since some of this conversation touched on the question of why my writing and my persona arouse hostility, the conjectures I gave you might be worth very little in fact.

Let's move from my private case to the general question of literary criticism. What should one expect from literary criticism? Is there still literary criticism?

In my dreams, a book review should be like a restaurant review: You read what a certain restaurant reviewer writes two or three or four times, and you go. If you see that her taste is nothing like yours, then you stop reading her. But if she happens to get it right time after time, and you discover that what she says is good really is good, then you'll follow her. That's the kind of book review I would like to see. Firstly, it should not purport to be the final, ultimate verdict. A review is not a Supreme Court ruling. It should say: I, the critic, appeal to readers who have some affinity with me, who have similar tastes, and then I sample things for them and I tell them: Watch out for this, try that, this one you should probably avoid.

I'm not sure you read restaurant reviews. They're just as cruel as book reviews.

That's true, I confess. I just idealized restaurant reviews because I'm simply not familiar with them. So, a correction: in a perfect world, I would like to find a restaurant reviewer and a book reviewer whose tastes are similar to mine, and so if she says "you should" or "you shouldn't," I could trust her to some degree, because our time and space will not suffice for us to try out all the world's restaurants and read all the books.

What No Writer Can Do

Hilit Yeshurun conducted a fascinating interview with you, in 1988.[8] Among other things, you told her that in *Where the Jackals Howl*, you marked your borders. Almost three decades have passed since that interview. I'm interested to know whether you still feel that's true.

I'll tell you something: I'm not even sure it was true when I told her that. No, I think I've been annexing territories all the time. I've never marked my borders. The language of the stories in *Where the Jackals Howl* is the highest Hebrew I had, and I never again wrote in such a high register. And that stemmed only from a lack of confidence: it was showing off, saying "look at me," look at my beautiful high vocabulary.

A decade later, you went back to that book and rewrote it.

Yes, I lowered it. So it would sound more like a person. So it wouldn't declaim. So there would not be that sort of showy extravagance.

That is the only time you did something like that.

The only time. Because I was barely twenty when I began the stories in *Where the Jackals Howl*, and I wanted people to know that I was proficient in biblical Hebrew and Mishnaic Hebrew and Talmudic Hebrew and Agnon Hebrew. I got over that. I wasn't the only one. A few new authors at the time felt the need to wear a swimsuit and a raincoat, gabardine trousers and blue work pants, all on top of each other. But no, *Where the Jackals Howl* did not mark my borders. Not at all. I think, for example, that in *The Same Sea* there are places I'd never been before. Not only in terms of the language and the words, but also in terms of the domains I entered. And when *Between Friends* came out, five or six years ago, I thought that would probably be the last piece of fiction I wrote, because I was stuck with *Judas*, I couldn't go on. And even though I used the same drawing of the kibbutz for the cover of *Between Friends* that had appeared on the first cover of *Where the Jackals Howl*, the distance between the former kibbutz stories and the latter ones is great, very great. In *Between Friends* I tell the stories in almost a whisper, compared to *Where the Jackals Howl*.

The truth is, when Hilit Yeshurun asked me about borders, and now you ask, I'm not exactly sure what borders are. I don't know why I said that to her. No, I don't stand behind that. I mean, I know roughly what things I can never do, what things I would like to do but am absolutely incapable of doing. A writer might be capable of writing about people who are more sensual than he or she. More tormented, uglier or more beautiful, richer or poorer. But no writer, anywhere or at any time, can write about a person more intelligent than him or her. It's impossible. Nor about a character with a better sense of humor. And those are my borders. Perhaps that is what I meant: I cannot write about a character smarter than me or about a character with more humor than I have. Absolutely not. Meaner? Certainly. Hungrier? More sated? More emotional? Hornier? Older? Younger? All those— yes. I have done so frequently. But smarter or funnier than I am—how can that be done?

I have the impression that over the years there's been more humor in your books. *A Tale of Love and Darkness*, whose tragic ending many readers remember, and which made me weep when I finished it, is, among other things, a very funny book. And that is true of other books you've written, particularly the later ones. Do you think that is a change you underwent as a writer?

Yes. My father had practically no sense of humor, nor did my mother. Father liked to make jokes a lot, but they were mostly "witticisms," "jests," or "puns," not living, spontaneous humor. All my children have a lot more humor than I do. My children's and grandchildren's sense of humor is also more refined and more sophisticated. Each one of them, in several different ways, has a keen sense for paradox, for wild exaggeration, but it's not mean humor. They poke fun at everything. They often poke fun at me. Sometimes I think my humor might come from my Uncle Zvi, Aunt Chaya's husband, even though we aren't related by blood. Uncle Zvi knew how to be witty, surprising, even jabbing, but never malicious. His son, my cousin Yigal, can also make us all roll around laughing. When I was a boy I envied them for being able to open their mouths and make people laugh. I didn't have that. I would gather all sorts of secondhand jokes and tell them to make people laugh. Mostly girls. But the girls didn't laugh at my jokes. Sometimes they laughed at me, but not at my jokes.

Yes, jokes aren't humor.

There is no humor in my early stories. None in the stories, and almost none in *My Michael*.

How do you explain the change? Is it a mechanism you cracked? Or is it that you're less reverential toward literature?

Perhaps you simply look at the world now and it seems funnier than it used to?

All the answers you suggested are correct, and they are not mutually exclusive. Except that instead of "reverential" I would say "tight-assed." That's how it was. When I started writing, yes, I was a tight-ass. I thought there were things that were simply beneath the dignity of literature. That was not my opinion of erotic things, or even incest. As early as *Where the Jackals Howl*, I wrote about incest and about erotic fantasies. But humor simply embarrassed me—what is this? Life isn't about having fun! Why should we laugh? Even when something amused me, I thought it wasn't appropriate for a written story. That changed. How? I don't know. I suppose something was buried all that time. When did it change? Perhaps it happened, paradoxically, after a near-fatal car crash in 1976, which left me with various impairments. Soon after that, I wrote a little children's book that was slightly funny, *Soumchi*. In that book I allowed myself to smile. Not quite to laugh but to smile and invite the reader to smile along with me.

Did you change in that way not only as a writer? I mean, do you think the world is funnier now, or that life is funnier?

Yes. I remember that my grandmother, the one who died of cleanliness, Grandma Shlomit, always used to say: "When you've already cried all your tears and you have none left to cry, it's a sign that it's time to start laughing." She also used to say that she had a terrible pain here and a terrible ache there and this hurt and that hurt and the other hurt, so much that it became funny. She would also say: "That person is so ugly, he's almost handsome." And also: "He's so educated, so erudite, so clever, that he doesn't understand anything."

Some things make us laugh because it's an automatic response, because there is an exaggeration. Because of what Bergson taught us, because "it hurts and hurts until it's funny."

Or else it's depressing.

Those are not contradictory. Comedy and tragedy are not two different planets. Chekhov, whom I like more and more—what is he? Funny or heartbreaking? Despairing or grinning? What is he? In one of Chekhov's plays there is a character, I think it's an old doctor, who's always sitting to one side mumbling, and every time he has a line, he repeats that two hundred years from now there will be completely different people living here, and they will not be able to understand why we were so miserable, because they'll always be happy, they'll always be healthy, full of joy and love, they will know how to live. He keeps saying that, and you can't understand why Chekhov gave a part to this nuisance who keeps repeating himself endlessly. But there is a moment in the play when one of the characters faints, and the old doctor examines her, and then looks up and says sadly: "I have forgotten everything."[9] In all of Shakespeare I have not found a more tragic phrase than those four words: "I have forgotten everything." They are funny and they break my heart: "I have forgotten everything." Incidentally, Chekhov called almost all his plays comedies. He insisted on it. People were astonished, they even mocked him a little. *Uncle Vanya* is a comedy? *The Seagull*? *The Three Sisters*? If those are comedies, then what is a tragedy? He insisted on calling them comedies and he fought with the directors, because he wanted people to laugh at his plays. When he watched his plays being performed and the audience didn't laugh even once, he saw it as an utter failure of the director and the actors. And a failure of his play.

Who else makes you laugh?

I think Shakespeare is funny sometimes in his tragedies, but it's not always understood. I taught *Othello* to high school juniors when I was a young teacher on Kibbutz Hulda, using Nathan Alterman's translation. And there is that horrible scene where Othello strangles Desdemona with his bare hands. And she dies. And then Emilia, Iago's wife, comes into the room: "Oh, who did that?" or something like that. And Desdemona murmurs, "Nobody; I myself. Farewell. Commend me to my kind lord. O, farewell!" The whole class burst out laughing, and rightly so: either Othello did strangle her or he didn't. If he strangled her to death, how is she making declarations? Did he or didn't he strangle her? I barked at the students: You should be ashamed of yourselves laughing at the most tragic point of the play! What's the matter with you? And then it happened again, and again. Every time I taught *Othello* in high school, and later at university, everywhere, after Othello strangles Desdemona and she says, "No one killed me," the class always burst out laughing. I finally understood that it's entirely possible that Shakespeare intended them to laugh. It is so horrible that it's funny. Shakespeare must have known they would laugh—what did he care if people laughed at the most tragic moment? I've found myself laughing at *Hamlet*, too. In the scene with the ghost, when he sees his father's ghost and says to it: Talk to me, talk to me, and the ghost says something like: I am the ghost of your miserable father, who was murdered by an impure hand. Now, when I remember it, I think Shakespeare deliberately gave the ghost such ceremonial words, so theatrical, turning it almost into parody. A bit of "play within a play." Or at the end of *Hamlet*, in the final scene, when everyone stabs or poisons everyone else, both the ones they meant to stab or poison and the ones they didn't.

I once sat in on a class you taught at Tel Aviv University on Agnon's "Fernheim." You essentially read the entire story to the class, and as you read you interpreted it. A close reading.

I taught literature for years, and my classes were almost always "close readings." I would bring a text to class—even *Only Yesterday*—and read the book with them from start to end, with a few omissions, and show them with my finger— look at this, look at that. Like the work of a tour guide who tells a group of tourists: Let's stop for a moment, look at the other side of the valley, remember that rock you see there, notice it. And two hours later, when they're on the other side of the valley, right under that rock, he says: Now I want you to look at the other side, where we were before, and understand why I told you to look here. That's roughly what I do. Simply because I've already taken that route several times and I know where we should stop and pay attention, and what is echoing up ahead and what is not. I did this when I taught high school and when I teach at university. I think most students come from love. Some of them might think I'm easy-listening, that I'm not serious enough, because I seldom use jargon, only in essential cases. Here and there I use the word "synthesis" or explain what an oxymoron is, that sort of thing, but much less than other teachers do. And when I do use the conventional terms, I give them a meaning that deviates slightly from the dictionary definition. For example, I explain "irony," in part, by using the phrase "false seriousness." To me, reading out loud is interpretation in and of itself, or at least it is more than half interpretation. I sometimes hear eye-opening things from students. I once read parts of *The Same Sea* in a university course, and there were students there who showed me things I hadn't seen. They have an association with something, something resembles something else, in the same book or in another book of mine, or in a book by someone else. Or something that happened to them in their own life. Those are the things that make my literature class. Even if it's a large auditorium—in Beersheba I sometimes had 140 or 150 students in my class—even then I would make sure people raised their hands and spoke. And if not everyone could hear the question or comment, I would repeat what they'd said over the microphone. I still enjoy doing that.

A lot of literature teachers make their students hate reading literature for the rest of their lives. Some of them come from the university, and they think their job in high school is to train a generation of scholars. But a high school literature teacher should not train scholars, just like a music teacher should not cultivate musicologists or composers. A music teacher seduces listeners and a literature teacher should seduce readers. I use the word "seduce" because I've always believed that education and teaching are a matter of seduction. Something almost erotic. The teacher aspires to make the students love something that he or she does. Yes. Seduction. In fact, education as seduction is Aristotle's idea. Have you ever thought about the fact that the Ministry of Education's jargon is full of verbs taken from the area of sexual violence?* Why not replace these verbs with ones from the domain of courtship, seduction, enchantment?

You like teaching.

I do. I like it and I enjoy it. But I always have the feeling that I'm leading my class along a narrow path between two craters. When you teach a literary work, or when you write a biography or a monograph of an author, it's very easy to fall into traps: for example, that the author's life explains the

---

* Oz cites several Hebrew terms as examples, which can be translated literally as: *penetrate, deepen, implant, open, dig in, insert, widen, sow.*

work. For example, that the author's life has nothing to do with the work. For example, that the poem simply reflects a certain experience of the writer. For example, that the poem does not express any experience of the author.

Teachers from the old generation used to ask: "What was the author trying to say?" They'd read Bialik's "Take Me under Your Wing," the most beautiful love poem in modern Hebrew literature, to my mind. Not since the Song of Songs has such a wonderful love poem been written in Hebrew. But the older generation of teachers would say: "What was the poet trying to say?" What does that question mean? One of three things: Either Bialik wanted to say something but because of difficulties expressing himself he was unable to do so, and so we—the teacher and the class together—will extricate the meaning out of his stutters and say what he would have said had he been able to express himself. Or, Bialik did say exactly what he wanted to, but in a foreign language, perhaps in Korean, and we must translate him into Hebrew. Or, Bialik is giving us a riddle, a Sudoku puzzle, or throwing a crossword at us, and we have to solve it and decipher it. "What was the poet trying to say?" But maybe he wasn't trying to say anything at all. Maybe he wanted to play music, or draw, or sing, or bark and howl at the moon, or act. Or all of those together.

Is that how you were taught literature too?

I had bad teachers and I had good teachers. I had Zelda. Zelda, the poet. There may never have been another literature teacher like her in the world. Ever. She was my teacher in second grade, and I was slightly in love with her, and she was the most wonderful teacher of words. What does a word do in a sentence? What does a word's position in a sentence do? How many pictures do you hang on the wall? And how much space do you leave between them? How important is the empty space between the pictures? Then we had a teacher at the religious school, Mordechai Michaeli; I can't even remember whether or not I wrote about him in *A Tale of Love and Darkness*. He used to pinch our cheeks. Never more than that, but he was an enthusiastic pincher. Mordechai Michaeli loved to tell stories. All class long he would tell us legends. Some were from Greek mythology, some from the Jewish sages and the legends of Israel, from various folktale anthologies. That's all disappeared now—who reads those things these days? Some of them must have been tales he made up himself, or combined, or turned upside down. He was supposed to be teaching literature, but he completely ignored the curriculum, he constantly told us legends. Three-quarters of the boys slept through his class, but Michaeli wasn't bothered at all. He never scolded or berated us. Another portion of the class would be throwing paper balls at each other, and that didn't bother him either: let them. But I sat there agape, my head always slightly tilted, my eyes wide, thirstily drinking in his stories. He simply told stories. He didn't analyze, didn't explain, didn't delve into the question of "What was the author trying to say?" He never offered us a moral, he didn't point to "artistic means" or "devices" or "mechanisms," nor did he elucidate the biographical or sociological or historical background. He let us off the hook when it came to context or morals, he simply told stories. And sometimes, only occasionally, at the end of the story or in the middle of it, he would repeat something he'd already said at the beginning, but the reiteration was a variation. A sort of twist. Or a little addition.

Later, at school on the kibbutz, we had a young teacher one year who was an outside employee they brought from the university, because there weren't enough teachers on the

kibbutz. He was a third-year student of Hebrew literature.
A refugee. A Holocaust survivor. I'm sure you know his
name: Aharon Appelfeld.

Aharon Appelfeld was extremely lacking in confidence in
those days, in every area. He taught us *Only Yesterday*: my
first encounter with that book, in eleventh or twelfth grade.
He taught well, he taught sensitively, but the thing is, he was
hesitant. Always hesitant. Always giving sideways glances to
see if he had a way out or somewhere to hide. He would say,
for example, "Summers in Palestine tend to be, in some ways,
much warmer than in Galicia." He had those sorts of reservations. Once he even said, "In certain respects Agnon was
not born in Israel." In class they made fun of him, but I always found Appelfeld's constant hesitation so touching.
Another teacher was the school headmaster, Ozer Huldai;
his son is now the mayor of Tel Aviv. Ozer Huldai was a
force of nature. He was one of the most charismatic people
I've ever met, and one of the most frightening. He could be
thunderous when he wanted to, and he sometimes made us
tremble. By vocation he was a science teacher; he taught biology and botany. But he also taught all the children to play
the recorder, and he gave history lessons, and showed us
slides of Renaissance art, and taught plant identification
using tweezers and a microscope, and sometimes he would
just get sick of everything and he'd walk into class and de-
clare, "Today we're going to talk about Napoleon all day!"
And this is how he would talk about Napoleon: in history,
in literature, in the German Romantics, in Beethoven's music,
in paintings. He would offer a broad overview, with large
aerial photographs. He wasn't a detail man, except in biology and botany. But his big aerial photographs are what I
will never forget. Where would you find, these days, a biology teacher who can teach a wonderful literature lesson?
There might be one or two left somewhere. Maybe.

Which of your university professors were especially influential on you?

Sadan, Halkin, and Shaked. Also Leah Goldberg, with whom I did not study but I sat in on a few of her lectures. She was sharp, acerbic, fascinating, very concise, she never waxed poetic in her lectures. Some of the philosophy teachers, too. Rotenstreich and Fleischmann, they were excellent teachers. Perhaps some of their kind are still around? I remember that Rotenstreich came into class the first day and posed a question: "What is the difference between a philosopher and a layman? The layman looks at a bridge and says to himself: that bridge is standing on pillars. The philosopher knows that the bridge is not standing on pillars, because bridges stand on laws, and if even one of the laws the bridge is standing on changes—the laws of geology, physics, metallurgy, hydrology, engineering—then all the piles will be worthless and the bridge will collapse like a deck of cards." That stays with me to this day. But my university studies were a blur, because I was already married to Nily and we already had Fania, and I used to travel to Jerusalem, spend two nights there, come back to Hulda, go back again, then back once more, and on top of that I had only two years to finish my undergraduate degree.

Because that's what the kibbutz allotted you?

The kibbutz was very cautious and suspicious: On the one hand, they urgently needed a literature teacher for the high school. They thought I was suitable, so they sent me to university. On the other hand, they were afraid that if I got my degree I'd probably leave the kibbutz as soon as I was finished, so they said: "Okay, you can study for two years and then come back to teach. Two years is enough for us, we don't need the degree, we don't insist on formalities." As it turned out, I got them twice: I earned my degree in two years, and I didn't leave the kibbutz.

When you went back, did you teach on the kibbutz?

Yes, I did. At first I taught three days a week, and on the other three I worked in the cotton, in the crops. At night I wrote stories, in the mornings I taught, on Saturdays I did "recruitments" in the fruit orchards, and in the evenings I did dining-room shifts. That is because thirty-five years ago the days and the nights were much, much longer than they are today, because Earth spun much slower, because at that time it wasn't yet orbited by all sorts of satellites.

Of course. There are other things that have changed, too. The way we read literature. The way we teach literature.

The instruction of literature in the past few decades has often turned into teaching the politics of minorities, or gender studies, or alternative narratives versus hegemonic narratives—in fact in many places they teach a type of sociology through literature. Oppressive discourse versus subversive discourse. Perhaps a combination of neo-Marxism with neo-Freudianism, with the occasional seasoning of Nietzsche.

A literary work strikes many people, perhaps including some at the Ministry of Education and Culture, as a sort of wagon that must carry a cargo to the students: the heritage of Eastern Jewry, or Holocaust awareness, or our entitlement to the country, or whatever. But when you read a good work of literature, the treasure is not in the depths of a safe that must be "cracked." The treasure is everywhere: in a single word. In the juxtaposition of words. In the punctuation. In the melody. In the repetitions. Everywhere. Above all, perhaps, it is actually in the spaces between the words or between the sentences or between the chapters.

Many people think that teaching literature means ripping off the mask or exposing the nudity. Not the nudity of reality, but the nudity of the story itself. For example, certain critics and scholars found in *My Michael* a plethora of offensive gender stereotypes. They found misogyny. They found the objectification of Hannah Gonen, the protagonist, and of the objects of her fantasies. They found loathsome Orientalism. They found racism. In short: they classified the book as an oppressive-racist text that represents the prejudices of a privileged white Jewish male. Hannah and I read some of the things that were written about us, and what we wish for our accusers is that their sexual fantasies always be absolutely politically correct.

Now they tell us that all the stories in the world, no matter the plot, the characters, the background, are in fact all the same story: a struggle for power and control. For hegemony. If you strip away the stories you will find, on one side, a privileged elite, and on the other, subversive oppressed people. Any story in the world, if you simply remove its peel, situates itself on either the good side or the bad side. Even a fairytale, a detective story, a joke, are not innocent. Scratch their surface and you will find exploitation and exclusion, constructs and brainwashing. Everything is didactic. Everything is for a cause. When this is the approach, teaching literature is like being an explosives specialist neutralizing a suspicious object, or a guerrilla fighter smuggling arms to oppressed peoples. Even an innocent fantasy is no longer innocent in our days, because the fantasizer is suspected of striving to "construct" his fantasy. To reproduce and impose it. To use it as an instrument of perpetuating the dominant hierarchy. Everyone is an agent: the characters, the author, the interpreting reader. The whole world is either paradigms or hogwash. All of literature is nothing but agendas or a cunning attempt to disguise agendas.

I disagree. I think these readings you are talking about can be brilliant and eye-opening, and sometimes they are truly path-breaking. Reading literature from the perspective of identity politics, for example, made a great contribution to our under-standing of literature itself and of the social and ideological systems in which it is written. It's true that sometimes this type of reading seems to have become a fad. And yes, some of these readings are not good: oversimplified, one-dimensional. They commit an injustice to the books. But there have always been embarrassing interpretations of literature and there always will be, assuming people continue to read.

Of course it is permissible and advisable to sometimes glimpse a story or a novel through a sociological or histori-cal lens, or out of political curiosity, or with psychological tools, or through feminist eyes. Anything goes. And some-times, as you say, it doesn't just go but it runs, and it's fasci-nating and it sheds new light, of course. Except that perhaps we should implement these observations without a demand for totality. Without a totalitarian steamroller. If a literary work is worth something, it is worth something precisely because it contains far more than can be siphoned into a so-phisticated container Model A or into a state-of-the-art container Model B. Also, in fact primarily, because we should not dispose of the "leftovers." If the reader or the critic, in their eagerness to expose the nudity, forgets the "leftovers," even the most cutting analysis might "darken as a room / without the stars left outside," as Alterman wrote.[10]

At least once a week someone from somewhere in the world comes to interview me. It always gets to the identical question stage, when they ask: "What is the role of litera-ture?" There are different variations: the role of literature in society, the role of literature in politics, in Jewish conscious-ness, in the Israeli-Palestinian conflict. And I tell these inter-viewers: "Change the question." Instead of asking me about the role of literature, ask me about the gift of literature. So they ask. Because they're polite. Because they feel bad. They're not satisfied, they want me to give them something juicy to put in the headline, they want to hear that literature is a whip that should be used on politicians, or that literature is the spearhead of revolution. I don't know what they want. Instead of all those, I say: the gift of literature. And I tell them it's a double gift. At first you read a novel or a story, and on page twenty-four you hold your breath: That is exactly me. How did this author know? She doesn't know me. She's not just talking about me, she's actually talking about my secrets, which I never told anyone. That is one kind of gift. The second is the opposite: you read page after page and you get to page eighty-four, and you are amazed: Wow, that could never be me. Even if they paid me a million dollars I would never do something like that. I am absolutely incapable of doing something like that. These two experiences: "That's exactly me" and "That could never be me" (and sometimes: "How lucky that isn't me") are among the great pleasures of reading, because you, the reader, are invited to reexamine your own borders. Including distant territories in the outer provinces that you seldom, or even never visit. But in the story you suddenly identify something and you say: Yes, I do have that remote region. I haven't been there for years, but it's mine, it's a part of me. Or the opposite: No. That is totally beyond my boundaries. I will never set foot there. Both things are a pleasure. And there is a third pleasure, which is that as you read, your borders begin to expand. The walls open up and you discover a landscape you've never seen before. Or a landscape you were afraid to see.

Here we are, back at the borders we started with.

Exactly. It is the pleasure of becoming acquainted. Acquainted with what? With both the familiar and the foreign.

I think they are both gifts. I won't tell you they are always a pleasure. Becoming acquainted with yourself is often the opposite of pleasure. And becoming acquainted with something foreign is also sometimes very difficult. But it is a gift. Everything suddenly expands. That, to me, is the gift of literature. And my delight as a storyteller is to give you a gift as a reader.

Perhaps that is the gift of all art, not just literature.

Good literature is far closer to painting and music than to history or sociology or Judaism or Zionism, to the heritage of Eastern and Western ethnicities, or whatnot. I might have already told you once that in my view, literature is actually the cousin of gossip, of the human thirst to know what is happening behind other people's shuttered blinds, to know what their secrets are. Except that literature doesn't say hello to this cousin of hers, gossip, when they meet on the street, because it is ashamed of their familial relations. The difference between these cousins is that gossip tells us what we already know: that everyone is actually the same and no one is all that great. Whereas literature sometimes tells us something we don't know, or something we always knew but didn't know we knew, and then it sheds a light that gives the familiar thing an exciting flavor of novelty, of the first time in our lives. Gossip is the eagerness we all have to peek through the neighbors' window and see whether or not they are more or less like us in there. In contrast, literature invites us sometimes to not only peek through the neighbors' window but to see, just for a moment, what the whole world looks like when you view it from the neighbors' window. And even what you and I look like when we are seen from the neighbors' window.

The Lights Have Been Changing without Us for a Long Time

We spoke about the changes you went through as a writer, for example the foot on the brake getting heavier. As a person, as a friend, as a political man, how do you think you have changed over the years?

That's pretty simple. Today I am far, far more forgiving than I was when I was twenty, or seventeen. I forgive far more. Except cruelty. I can forgive a lot of things, but not cruelty. I'll say something now that I'm not sure of: perhaps this change makes me a slightly better writer. Why am I not sure of this? Because there have been writers who have written cruelly, by writing about cruelty with seemingly no forgiveness or compassion. Samuel Beckett, for example, or even Kafka. They wrote without compassion. So perhaps this should not be turned into a generalization. I'm saying, just for myself, that forgiveness might have made me a slightly better author, in my way.

I will qualify your qualification: if I'm not mistaken, Beckett and Kafka are writers you feel less of an affinity with. Is that true?

With Kafka more, with Beckett less. I feel an affinity with Kafka for many reasons. Less so with Beckett. Kafka even hangs on my wall in here. Did you see him by the doorway? His Hebrew exercises?

Unlike Chekhov and Agnon and others, we've never spoken of him, so I mistakenly assumed he was less close to you.

Then we will speak of him. But before we speak of Kafka, I want to tell you a story about our friend Eran Dolev, director of a ward at Ichilov Hospital. He once told us that a woman of 102 was brought to the hospital with a hand injury. They bandaged her up in the ER and told her to go upstairs and see a specialist, because she was 102. Our friend examined her and found that she was absolutely fine. He asked her: Where are you going from here? She said: Home. Where is home? Jaffa. How do you get there? I take two buses. He said: You know what? I've finished my shift, I'll drive you home. On the way he asks her: Do you have children? She says: Yes, two sons. Where are they? In assisted living. It turns out that twice a week she takes the bus from Jaffa to two different assisted living facilities to bring her children the food they like. I say this so that you, as a mother, will know that "from our struggle only death can free us."* I just liked that story so I wanted to tell it to you. How is it related to Kafka? Perhaps because in *The Metamorphosis* the father is always terrible, malicious, destructive, heartless. The mother only becomes that way later, and the sister is the last to give up on the monster that appears in their home. She takes pity on him, but her compassion slowly runs out, just as patience runs out, and in the end she is also happy that he dies. In the end the whole family goes from slavery to freedom and from darkness to great light. The whole claustrophobic story ends suddenly with the liberated family going out into nature, to blue skies and verdant hills. Perhaps that is a different sort of compassion. Perhaps.

------

* From a poem by underground fighter Avraham Stern (known as "Yair"), entitled "Nameless Soldiers."

We started talking about the ways you've changed, and I didn't give you the chance to answer because we switched to Kafka.

There was a period that ended when I was still very young, when here in Israel writers and poets had a great influence on public life. Bialik and Brenner, Shlonsky and Alterman, Uri Zvi Greenberg, S. Yizhar, Moshe Shamir. Politicians sought their company, public opinion valued them. Why was that? I don't know, perhaps it's some sort of Judeo-Slavic tradition. That sort of thing could never happen in the English-speaking world. I'm not sure American presidents know who the most interesting American poets of their time are. Obama certainly does, but take Trump, or George Bush—if you held a gun to his head and asked, "Who is the most interesting American poet? You have ten seconds to an-swer," he'd say, "Shoot, don't waste the ten seconds."

In revolutionary times, in times of great change, it some-times happens that large parts of the public are attentive to the voices of a small handful of literary figures, poets or novelists or philosophers. When normal times resume, that ends. In Russia the period we're speaking of, when Russian poetry and literature might have provided a smoke signal for all of Russian history, lasted roughly from the middle of the nineteenth century until the fall of Communism, a little less. Because even in the Communist period some poets and writ-ers sent out smoke signals to dissidents. But that is only in revolutionary times. Then come other times, when there is a certain ritual of listening to poets and writers, yes, the ritual still continues a little, but it is almost devoid of content. Meaning, writers still stand at the street corners and clap their hands every minute and a half, and perhaps some of them believe that all the traffic lights in the city change be-cause they clapped their hands, but that has not been the case for a long time. It's been years since it made much difference what a poet claimed or what a writer shouted, but the ritual continues, or it did until a few years ago. Here I am, standing at the intersection, full of self-importance, expecting the lights to change when I clap. There are quite a few people who mock me, and they are probably right.

But still, your opinion is solicited. You are invited to speak, to write in the papers.

And prime ministers have sometimes asked me over for personal talks, sometimes not even in their office but at home, for a drink, or coffee, depending on which prime minister it is. Dinner and a heart-to-heart, with questions like "Where did we go wrong?" and "Where do we go from here?" They often admire your answers but they always ignore them completely. And almost all of them—not Ben-Gurion, but Golda and Eshkol and Shamir and Peres—tell me: "How you phrase things! Such Hebrew! Such oratorical skills! You're wrong, but you put it so well!" Once in my life, just once, I would like to have a prime minister say: "Amos Oz, you talk like shit, you phrase things terribly, the words don't stick together, but you know what? You're right." I would like to hear just that before I leave.

Has it never happened?

Never. The lights change without us now. Younger writers, the generation after Haim Be'er, David Grossman, Meir Shalev, and Yitzhak Laor, most of them have already understood this and they hardly even try. They don't even try to raise their voices. They don't want to make fools out of themselves. Once or twice I've heard Etgar Keret speak out in the papers, or Nir Baram, Dorit Rabinyan, Iris Leal. There are a few groups of young poets, maybe someone else here and there, but others not at all. It's gone. We dinosaurs, Yehoshua and I, keep it up once in a while, as does Grossman.

I once wrote a sort of parable that I took from an age-old story: In London, decades ago, they still had that phenomenon of the smog. There is air pollution now, too, but back then the city was completely black and there were days when you couldn't leave the house because it was impossible to breathe or see. Even if you shone a flashlight on your hand, you couldn't see it. And the story is about a man who was told on the phone that his wife was giving birth in a hospital on the other side of town and there was a complication and he had to come. So off he goes, and there's not a soul on the streets. No cars, no taxis, no pedestrians. He stands in the thick darkness and calls out: Help me! A stranger comes over and our man explains the situation, and the stranger takes his arm and says, Turn left here, now turn right, watch out here, there's a step. The stranger takes our man all the way to the hospital. Our man thanks the stranger, hugs him in the dark, because he can't see him, and asks: "How could you, in this total darkness, how could you navigate?" And the stranger says: "The dark doesn't bother me. I'm blind." There are times when, at least in some places, a poet can suddenly be this sort of blind man showing the way, because he is an expert in darkness. But in normative situations, when there is light on the street and there are taxis and buses and this and that, who needs a blind man to show us the way?

Interesting. I asked you how you have changed, and you told me how the ground has moved.

No, it affects me too. My passion to sit down and write a political op-ed has diminished. This morning I wanted to write a piece, but I didn't. It's not completely gone, the passion, I still write op-eds from time to time. But less. I used to write out of anger. Almost every week I had an opinion piece in the paper. Sometimes even twice a week. I wrote for *Davar*, for *Yediot Aharonot*, for *Haaretz*, and several major newspapers overseas translated and published every word. Or sent troupes of interviewers. Now that market stall is closed. It opens temporarily and infrequently.

Is that because you think people listen to you less?

Yes. The truth is that this phenomenon of influence is a profound mystery to me. I've never understood what influence actually is. I sometimes see strangers, or myself, in a restaurant, order the fish and a second later call the waiter back and say, No, you know what? I'll have the chicken today, not the fish. What went through their mind? What went through my mind? I don't know. Nor does the man who changed his order. It's a profound mystery. I've never heard that in the Knesset—even when there were still great speechmakers—I never heard a member from the opposing party get up and say: "I listened to your speech and my eyes were opened; I realized you are right." Never happened. There are hundreds of volumes of Knesset protocols, but you won't find that line in them. Nor in the courts. In all the annals of the courts in all the world it has never once happened that a defense lawyer or a prosecutor got up after the opposing lawyer's arguments and said: "I have heard my distinguished colleague's arguments and I am persuaded that he is right and I am simply mistaken."

I have never had the experience of someone coming up to me and saying, "I read you and I was reborn." "I heard your speech, I saw your television interview, there's no two ways about it, you're right." That hasn't happened to me. I don't know whether the conclusion is that words have no effect, or that people don't like to admit they've been influenced. Israelis are especially reluctant to admit that they've changed their minds. Israeli men in particular. An Israeli man will sometimes tell you something that is 180 degrees contradictory to what he told you a year ago. But if you express sur-

prise and say, "But just one year ago you said the exact opposite," he'll reply, "What are you talking about? A year ago
I said exactly what I'm saying now, you just misunderstood
me." By the way, I stopped giving TV interviews a few years
ago because I realized that when I speak about the State of
Israel being in grave danger, the next day a lot of people,
strangers and not strangers, stop me on the street and eagerly
exclaim: "What's the matter with you? How could you? Are
you out of your mind? Don't ever wear that sweater on television again!" Well, I decided to give up TV appearances, but
I did not give up on that sweater.

You cannot measure influence. Even if it exists, there is no
way in the world to measure it, and don't let any sociolo-
gists tell you they can, because they can't. Take the idea of
two states, of independence for the Palestinians. In '67 there
were so few people who supported it that you could have
held a national conference of all supporters of a Palestinian
state alongside Israel inside a phone booth. Almost. Today
there are a few million Israelis and perhaps also a great many
Palestinians who think that while the idea may not be that
great, there is simply no other way. That did not happen
under the influence of me and my friends, but because of a
few reality strikes: intifadas, bloodshed, international isola-
tion, demographic fears—many things did it, but not my and
my friends' op-eds. And if lately there are more and more
people on both sides despairing of the two-state solution,
that also did not happen because someone raised a good argument, but because of a few reality strikes that make some
people think the situation is "irreversible."

But you think the situation is reversible.

Yes. There is a way to reach a compromise between the two
nations who live in this land, and the compromise is to di-
vide the land into two neighboring states. But lately I think

that it won't do any good for me to keep repeating that. My world used to be divided into three groups: the people who were convinced I was more or less right, to whom there was no need to talk; the people convinced with absolute certainty that I'm terrible, or I'm a nutcase, or I'm a traitor and an enemy of the Jews, and I have nothing to say to them either; and then there were the people who were willing to listen because they weren't completely sure what to do. Those were the ones I always spoke to. The open-minded ones. The ones who were not entrenched. The ones not ashamed to be persuaded. In fact I always tried to speak to Edith, the wife of Archie Bunker, who was a sort of neighborhood Donald Trump. Because Archie will always be a racist, he'll always want to settle everything by force. Gloria, their daughter, and Michael, her husband, are always moderate and enlightened, and only Edith, whom many remember as a ridiculous fool, is actually open to being persuaded, sometimes this way and sometimes the other. To me she is not a fool at all, and she is the person I addressed in my articles, she is the one I spoke to when I still gave interviews or got into arguments on television. To this day, I think the opposition should mostly address Edith. Not to provoke her, not to shock or humiliate her, not to condescend to her, but to look her in the eye and talk to her.

In fact the world is still divided into the three groups, but I think I am less and less able to reach the people who are not completely resolved on one of the ends. There are some, the minority, who agree with my opinions, and there is no point in me telling them again and again things they know very well. They know that Israeli society is built on many injustices, that the rich are getting richer and the poor are getting trampled. They know that the occupation corrupts, that the Supreme Court is important, that without the rule of law we will be ruled by mafia gangs, they know it's wrong to rob land, and that oppression breeds hatred. They know it's very dangerous to go against the whole world. But there are also people who have one part of their brain guiding them to moderation, to humanism, to compromising with the Palestinians, but another part warning them that there's no one to talk to, that the Arabs only want to slaughter us all, that making compromises and concessions in return for peace is a trap, that anyone who makes concessions is a sucker. Those people, who are still hesitant, maybe they can still be reached, but not by me. They wouldn't even read what I write. There has to be a different voice. A different language. A different generation. Not the voice of a privileged old Ashkenazi writer who still gives off a whiff of kibbutzim and the labor union and Peace Now and the handsome young pioneers.

That takes me back to something I said at Yossi Sarid's funeral: it is not up to us to finish the job. Others will come. Younger men and women will come. A new generation of people who believe in peace and social justice will come, and they may have a different language and perhaps different modes of persuasion and different arguments than ours. And they may find the way to reach the hearts of millions of Israelis who have not agreed with us up to now. Not because they're all racists or hate-filled and brainwashed, definitely not, but because many of them are genuinely worried and genuinely afraid, although they are open to different voices than my own and to different arguments. Maybe.

Yet you did publish a book of political essays, in which you hoped to speak partly—or, as we wrote on the back cover—primarily, to readers whose opinions differ from yours.

In *Dear Zealots* I try, for a change, to speak softly. To quietly say things I once used to shout. Does that guarantee me new listeners? I don't know. Sometimes being soft-spoken is actually what provokes anger and aggression in one's antagonists. That happens even in family quarrels: if the first party yells and rages and the second party listens quietly and reasonably, the first party does not calm down but on the contrary, he becomes even angrier and more offended. Sometimes.

In that book I primarily address readers who identify with religious Zionism, because I have the vague sense that perhaps the next wave of Hebrew literary creation and of innovative Israeli thought will come from, among other places, the world of the settlers. Many letters that I receive from settlers indicate both disquiet and awareness.

It seems to me that you are trying not to ridicule beliefs and opinions you once ridiculed.

Over the years I've been losing the urge to disparage beliefs and opinions I find baseless. People who believe in miracles, for example, or in amulets, or holy burial sites. I am gradually losing my urge to denounce them, because the world is a pretty terrible place and life does not end well. All of our lives end with decline, disease, dementia, death—things don't end well. There is usually a lot of suffering, disappointment, and loss. So why should I care if a person finds some comfort in kissing an amulet? Or prostrating himself on a rabbi's grave? If this person tried to force me to kiss amulets, I would refuse and I would be outraged. But he's not forcing anyone. There are millions of Jews who kiss mezuzahs, or kiss the stones of the Western Wall. There are hundreds of millions of Christians who cross themselves several times a day, including a lot of secular people. So let them cross themselves. Let them kiss stones. What do I care?

After the siege of Jerusalem, in September 1948, the first coin minted by the State of Israel reached us from Tel Aviv: the 25-*pruta* coin. It was an enormous aluminum coin, almost the size of a little figurine, and I think there were stalks of grain on the flip side. My grandfather, Alexander, who was loved by women and was a secular Revisionist and a great hedonist, picked up the coin, kissed it, and said a blessing to "He who has kept us alive, sustained us, and brought us to this season." He passed it around the circle of people in our courtyard, and they also kissed the coin and excitedly recited the *She'hecheyanu* blessing. I don't kiss coins anymore. What am I, crazy? Who kisses coins? My children don't kiss coins and neither do my grandchildren. But perhaps the fact that I don't kiss coins is only because my grandfather was fortunate enough to kiss that Hebrew coin, the first after two thousand years. Perhaps he kissed the coin on my behalf, too, and on behalf of the children and grandchildren and great-grandchildren. He certainly kissed it on behalf of his parents and forefathers. I, for example, sometimes kiss pictures of my children and grandchildren from when they were little. Sometimes I look at one of those pictures and I feel a surge of emotion, and I kiss it. So what? Does that hurt anyone? Every person in the world ought to find something that comforts him, even if in someone else's view it is a comical or silly comfort. I hardly know anyone who doesn't have a couple of superstitions. Including secular people, including myself. I'm not asking you, but ask yourself whether you do.

I have lots—knock on wood. What are your superstitions?

No, no, that's private, I don't want to talk about it. But I would never mock anyone for their superstitions, as long as they don't harm others, and as long as they don't try to coerce me into doing things I don't want to do and don't believe in.

You spoke of how limited the influence of your words has been, but your books, certainly some of them, do have a great effect on people. We've already discussed *A Tale of Love and Darkness*, which had a profound effect on many readers. My father is one of them. It's not the kind of influence you're talking about, but a different kind.

There should be a different word for it in Hebrew.

Yes. I think the first kind is what would be called "influence" in English, and the second kind is . . .

Impact. Maybe Hebrew should distinguish between someone who "influences" and someone who "leaves a mark."

I like that.

I'm glad you're asking this. I focused on "influence" in the sense of causing people to change their mind. That is what I said is mysterious. There are books, and movies, that have changed my life. There's Bach's Cantata BWV 106: the first time I heard that, I knew I would never again be the same exact person. That happened to me with *Crime and Punishment*, and with short stories by Sherwood Anderson, with Berdyczewski, with Chekhov. It happened with Agnon's *A Simple Story*, and other things he wrote, although interestingly his love stories rather than the great novels. Of course I believe that's happened to other people. I know it has. Yes. A book or a film or a piece of music can change us. Someone who has never in his life been changed in any way by a book or a film or a picture or music is—a squandered person. And it's not just art. There are people who are profoundly changed by travel. I think almost everyone. For example, I think that anyone who hasn't ever spent real time, not tourist time with a camera, but real time in a foreign country, cannot understand their own country. Someone who does not speak at least one foreign language does not understand their own language. I even think that only on one's second love does one begin to understand one's first love. I think so. Things may often influence not your future acts, but a new understanding of the familiar. That is influence in the sense of making an impact, leaving a mark—I'm glad you corrected me. You've influenced me and I even admit it. A miracle.

I'll correct you and say that I didn't exactly correct you.

You expanded what I said. You did. Travel, love, encounters—of course they change us. I was speaking about influence in the narrow sense, as in when people change their mind, and I told you that was hard to quantify. I did not say that it doesn't happen but that it's hard to quantify, because even when people do change their mind, they usually doesn't like to admit it. And I said that perhaps in times of revolution you can see books or words that propel people. I've written about five or six hundred articles in my life, more or less, I haven't kept count. Had I known they wouldn't budge even a single voter, I still would have written them. And I would have gone to meetings of Meretz, and before that Moked, and Sheli, and Peace Now, and the Committee for Peace and Security—I would have gone even if I'd known it didn't move a single voter. I would have gone. Out of a certain compulsion, a sense of civic duty. But when people ask me: "How much influence have you had?" "How much influence have all of you had?" I'm not sure that can be measured. As Stalin asked at Yalta: "How many divisions does the Pope have?" And the answer is that military divisions are very influential and so are ideas. But the influence of divisions is easily measured, whereas the influence of ideas—I don't know of a way to measure that.

I don't think I've ever heard you say anything, or read anything you've written, from which a sense of despair arose. Don't you ever despair?

I feel fear. Mostly I fear the rise of fanaticism of all kinds. I do not despair, because I don't know what will happen.

Terrible things might happen, but good things might happen too, things that no one can conceive of. Almost all the events that changed reality throughout my life have been unexpected. Sudden. The Six-Day War. The Yom Kippur War. Sadat's visit and peace with Egypt. The collapse of Communism. The Oslo Accords. The assassination of Rabin. The destruction of the Twin Towers in New York. The evacuation of settlers from Gaza. Each of those events happened unexpectedly. I don't despair because I know that living is like driving a car with the windshield completely covered, and all you have is the side-view mirrors reflecting what is behind you. We only know what has happened, not what awaits us. Don't get me wrong, it's not that I'm an eternal optimist. On certain matters I am pessimistic. But perhaps my pessimism is sweetened by the fact that I like people and find them fascinating. I do not have an iota of misanthropy.

That's true.

Even when someone makes my blood boil, I am no longer filled with hatred. Pessimism—yes. Quite often I think things will not go well. For example, the fact that your son is growing up in a world that uses "texting" language. Where if people read literature at all, they will only read very short texts, and the monumental brainwashing inflicted on us by advertisers will keep telling them: Throw out everything that's old, buy new. A lot of people already say: "Who needs the past? That's not interesting. Why do I need to know who Herzl was, or Ben-Gurion, or Shakespeare? Only what's new is worth anything." That is not a good sign. Mostly, I'm not optimistic when I see, in many places in the world, the victory of a right wing brimming with hate and fear, and conversely a left wing that is often banal, naïve, establishment-hating, hostile toward anyone who is powerful and hegemonic. The blanket that I spread over all these things, starting with the erasure of the past and all the way to the political developments occurring now, the common denominator among the simplistic right and the naïve left, is that politics and media are becoming branches of the entertainment industry. Problems are portrayed as gags. Solutions as text messages. Life as a gimmick. I'm talking about the systematic infantilization of humanity.

Given all that, how can you still love humankind?

I love humankind because men and women have been kind to me. And perhaps because I did not have a good childhood, which meant that I learned to be grateful every time anyone did something kind for me.

I hear you say that a lot, that you are grateful.

I am grateful for you and me having met and that we work together.

So am I.

Many times, Shira, I am grateful when someone talks to me, and grateful when someone listens to me. Neither of those things can be taken for granted. Do you know how many people around us, right now, while the two of us sit here talking, have no one to listen to them? No one who wants to listen to them or talk to them except advertisers? Masses. Masses. Not only lonely, elderly people in assisted living, not only people with no family. No. Even in bustling homes, even in families, there are so many. No one really wants to talk to them except to say "put," "bring," "take," "don't forget." And no one wants to hear them. So it's not a given that you are talking to me and listening to me here now, and I to you. It's a gift.

Does old age preoccupy you? Death?

A while ago I was invited to give a lecture at a medical-science conference, on the topic of "end of life." They asked me to talk about hope and despair, and about suicide, and about love and darkness. Because after all I'm considered an expert on love, an expert on darkness, and an expert on suicide. I asked them, and I asked myself, and now I ask you: Why are we so afraid of death? Some of us more so, some a little less, but we're all afraid of it. After all, the world existed for billions of years before we were born, without us, and it will continue to exist for billions of years after we're gone—again, without us. We are a sort of flicker, a passing twinkle. And if that is the case, then why is the black abyss after death so frightening to us? What is the difference, in fact, between the black abyss before our life began and the one after it ends? I have no answer, of course, but the mere question helps me a little when I think about death. Because in fact I've already been there, in that black abyss of utter oblivion, before I was born. I was there for millions of years, and things weren't that bad for me. Why would it be so bad to be there again?

There is a verse in the Book of Job that people have been repeating for thousands of years, but almost no one stops to listen—in astonishment, in fear and trepidation—to the actual words: "Naked came I out of my mother's womb, and naked shall I return thither." We repeat it just like that, casually, as if the moral is: don't keep running around buying and acquiring and amassing and investing, because you're not taking any of that with you to the grave. But the verse does not say, "Naked came I out of my mother's womb, and naked shall I go to my grave." It is not at all a statement about the folly of accumulating assets. In fact it's a far more sensational verse. It promises us that after death we return to exactly the place we left: our mother's womb. No less. And the place we left was, after all, pretty good. So perhaps death really isn't that bad: leave the womb, make a bit of noise over here, run around, buy stuff, travel, go home, love, make an impression, be impressed, be disappointed, then just back to the womb? Fine, why not. There, in the womb, we are cared for, we are wrapped in warmth and tenderness, we are fed, and we have no worries. This verse from Job is worth a second look, because it enfolds a wonderful promise. More wonderful, perhaps, than the Behemoth and the Leviathan of the Jewish paradise, more than the seventy-two virgins of the Muslim paradise.

Aren't you afraid of death?

The things I'm telling you now are the things I tell myself precisely when I am trembling with the fear of death. And even if I am able to believe in that verse for a moment, the fear doesn't go away. Even then, I'm not willing to die this evening or tomorrow morning, happy and peaceful. Of course not. Because, all things considered, I'm having a very interesting time here. Even the terrible and horrifying things are interesting. I'd be sad to miss out. I am so curious to find out what happens. If someone were to tell me: You won't be here soon, but up there you'll have a balcony with large telescopes where you can sit and keep an eye on your kids and grandkids, I might agree. I would say: Okay, then I won't eat and I won't drink and I won't put on clothes, but sometimes I will hear music and at least I'll know what's going on. I'll still be in the picture.

You won't be able to take action either.

I won't be able to take action, that's true. I can't take much action now, either, so maybe it won't be such a big change. Alterman, in *The Joy of the Poor*, writes: "For the world is divided / in two / and its murmured eulogy is twofold, / for there is not a home without dying, / and the dead shall forget not their home."[11] When we talked about *A Tale of Love and Darkness*, I think I told you that I wrote that book, among other reasons, to invite the dead back home and in-troduce them to Nily and my children and grandchildren, to talk to them, to ask them some questions, to show them a few surprises, then send them back where they belong, so they won't live in our home. I definitely don't want them living with us. That, to me, is the only way to live with the dead: to invite them over sometimes, make them a cup of coffee, reminisce a little with them, try to reconcile with them a little, and then send them back to the darkness. They can wait patiently for us there, because after all we still have a couple of things we need to take care of. And the light is still so sweet to our eyes.

ACKNOWLEDGMENTS

Our thanks to all who read the manuscript of this book, commented, cautioned, and improved.

—*Amos Oz and Shira Hadad*

Nily Oz
Amir Hadad
Charles Buchan
Ernit Cohen-Barak
Rivka Fendreich
Nurit Gertz
Zvia and Mark Glazerman
Ayelet Gundar-Goshen
Aviad Kleinberg
Niva Lanir and Giora Morag
Gafnit Lasri-Kukya
Dror Mishani
Roni Modan
Yael Neeman
Ran Nitzan
Yifat Nitzan
Haim Oron (Jumes)
Daniel Oz
Fania Oz-Salzberger
Aliza Raz Melzer
Yonatan Sagiv
Ali Salzberger
Ada Vardi
A. B. Yehoshua

NOTES

Some of the quotes in the book are provided as they appear in their original sources, while others we have chosen to keep as they were imprinted in the speakers' memories and appeared in our conversations.

1. *Sounds, Feelings, Thoughts: Seventy Poems by Wisława Szymborska*, trans. Magnus J. Krynski and Robert A. Maguire (Princeton University Press, 1981).
2. A. B. Yehoshua, *Three Days and a Child*, trans. Miriam Arad (Doubleday, 1970).
3. Pinchas Sadeh, "On the Margins of the Little Chronicle of Anna Magdalena," in *For Two Distinguished Girls* (Schocken, 1977), 25.
4. Assaf Inbari, "Be Thankful for That Which Is Complete," *Eretz Acheret*, no. 49, January–February 2009.
5. S. Y. Agnon, *T'mol Shilshom* (Schocken, 1966), 211.
6. Yigal Schwartz, *The Soulful Song of Amos Oz: The Cult of the Writer and the Religion of the State* (Kinneret-Zmora-Bitan-Dvir, 2011), 9–10.
7. Aviad Raz, "Why We Love to Hate Amos Oz: Reflections Following the Latest Collective Attack," *Haaretz*, March 3, 1989.
8. Hilit Yeshurun, *How Did You Do It? Interviews from "Rooms"* (Hakibbutz Hameuchad, 2016), 189–228.
9. The play is *The Three Sisters*. The character who discusses the people who will live in two hundred years is Lieutenant-Colonel Vershinin, while the doctor, Chebutykin, is the one who says, "I have forgotten everything," or, "I remember nothing," when recalling a patient who died because of him. The quote is given here as it appeared in our conversation.
10. Nathan Alterman, "Endless Encounter," in *Stars Outside* (Hakibbutz Hameuchad, 1995), 9.
11. Nathan Alterman, "The Mole," in *The Joy of the Poor* (Mahbarot Le'Sifrut, 5717), 17.